Mamie Cadden
Backstreet Abortionist

Mamie Cadden photographed with her
MG sportscar in the Phoenix Park in 1938
Photograph © Atlantic Syndication

Mamie Cadden
Backstreet Abortionist

Ray Kavanagh

MERCIER PRESS

Mercier Press
Douglas Village, Cork
Email: books@mercierpress.ie
Website: www.mercierpress.ie

Trade enquiries to CMD Distribution
55A Spruce Avenue, Stillorgan Industrial Park
Blackrock, County Dublin
Tel: (01) 294 2560; Fax: (01) 294 2564
E-mail: cmd@columba.ie

A CIP record for this title is available
from the British Library

Cover photograph reproduced with
kind permission of the National Archives

Mercier Press receives financial assistance from the Arts Council/An Chomhairle Ealaíon

Printed in England by J H Haynes & Co. Ltd

Contents

Acknowledgements

I gratefully acknowledge the assistance and courtesy shown to me by the following in the preparation of this work:

Stanley Siev, solicitor to Miss Cadden in the 1956 trials; Greg O'Connor and the staff at the National Archives; Dr Sandra McAvoy, scholar on the history of abortion in twentieth-century Ireland; the staff of the National Library of Ireland; Gavin Corbett, who allowed me to use his dissertation on Miss Cadden; Muiris MacGonigal, schoolboy friend of Miss Cadden; Brendan Ashe; Gerry Callanan; Mary Flynn; Cllr Michael Conaghan; Cllr Eamonn Maloney; Mary Thornton; Dr Bill Vaughan; Cathal O'Shannon; Ted Sheehy; Sergeant Patrick McGee of the Garda Museum; Tim Cadogan of Cork County Library; Pa Barry of Conna; members of the Cadden family; the staff of Kevin Street Public Library; the British Library Newspaper Library; and those friends and relatives of Miss Cadden who don't want their names mentioned.

Prologue

From the start I wanted to get to know Mamie Cadden. I wanted to know how she felt about her tormentors, about her life, and the Ireland in which she lived. Obviously this would be a difficult task in relation to her earliest years as most of her contemporaries are dead and written sources are few.

The same was not true for her final years in the 1950s. Many who witnessed her final humiliations and who spoke to her before her trial for murder in 1956 are still alive; there are extensive newspaper accounts and her comments and outbursts are well recorded; the transcripts of the court witnesses are also available. From these I constructed an account of what happened in her cramped bedsit in Hume Street on the days after the death of Helen O'Reilly and before Mamie's arrest. The words are her own and around them it was possible to deduce the rage, doubts, recriminations and hopes that were part of her last few days of freedom. These make up the first chapter of the book. The rest of the book, though based on extensive research, lacks the firsthand witness accounts that were available to me for her final few years.

Mamie Cadden was a truly remarkable woman whose life in many ways mirrored the new state in which she lived. As she approached the end of her life so too was the life of the narrow-minded, isolationist, confessional and hypocritical society in which she lived ending. As the 1960s dawned, with its opening up of Ireland to outside influences and material prosperity, the other Ireland was disappearing and soon, like Mamie Cadden, would be relegated to history.

– Ray Kavanagh

Chronology

1891 Mary Anne Cadden is born in Scranton, Pennsylvania, the eldest child of an Irish emigrant couple.

1895 The family returns to Mayo, takes up farming and establishes a small grocery business.

1911 The homestead is purchased from the landlord and part of it put in Mamie's name.

1925 Mamie leaves Mayo and settles in Dublin.

1926 She qualifies as a midwife after a course in the National Maternity Hospital, Dublin (Holles Street).

1929 She opens her first nursing-home at 61 Lower Beechwood Avenue in Ranelagh.

1931 She buys and opens her own nursing-home, St Maelruin's, in Rathmines.

1938 Mamie is charged with 'child abandonment' along with her maid, Molly O'Grady.

1939 She is sentenced to a year's hard labour in Mountjoy Jail.

1940 She re-establishes her business at Upper Pembroke Street

1945 She is convicted of 'procuring a miscarriage'; sentenced to five years penal servitude in Mountjoy Jail.

1950 On her release Mamie re-establishes her business in Hume Street.

1951 The body of Brigid Breslin is found on Hume Street.

1956 The body of Helen O'Reilly is found on Hume Street; Mamie is charged and convicted with her murder and sentenced to hang.

1957   Mamie's sentence is commuted to life imprisonment
and she commences her term in Mounjoy Jail.

1958   Mamie is declared insane and transferred to the
Criminal Lunatic Asylum in Dundrum.

1959   Mamie dies of a heart attack in custody in Dundrum.

1

The Poor Bitch

9.30 a.m., Wednesday, 18 April 1956

'Damn them all! I'm in flames!' she muttered as she banged the breakfast dishes down on the table. 'They won't get me on this one.' Sitting at the table in her red dressing-gown she glared around her miserable pokey flat at 17 Hume Street near Dublin's St Stephen's Green. 'And that bastard of a landlord, Laurence Brophy, and his grasping wife, Gertrude – I'll cook their goose: that letter to the revenue commissioners will make him think twice before he tries to push Mamie Cadden around again.[1] A bloody rent increase for this dive? He wants to get me out, that's what he wants. It's against the law; my bloody rent is fixed by the court.' She chuckled when she thought of the revenue commissioners investigating the affairs of her landlord in his so-called South City Hotel at 24 South Great George's Street. 'Hotel my arse,' she thought. 'It's a bloody guest-house. I bet he doesn't pay a halfpenny tax on that either. Bloody Irish Catholic landlords, beggars on horseback that's what they are; worse than the Protestant ones, and at least the Prods have some class, not like the Brophys.

'Well, I've told the revenue commissioners who was really with me on that night in Meath in June 1938 when that child was abandoned. It's about time the bloody truth came out. And I've told them who paid for Ellen Thompson's abortion in 1944. They're such hypocrites but it will be all over Dublin in a week; they won't be able to keep their mouths shut.'

She reached over to the stove for the teapot and the stinging pain of arthritis shot up her right arm. She hadn't been in top form for a few days what with the arthritis and Brophy trying to kick her out of her flat. Still, she had enjoyed writing the letter to the revenue, even if her handwriting was not like it used to be. She thought about an article she had seen in the *Daily Mail* about a cure for arthritis in the Canary Islands: 'I'll go in the summer. That'll give them all something to talk about.'

She patted her mass of dyed blonde hair before taking some more tea. 'And then there's bloody Helen O'Reilly, Miss Blackcoat, or whatever her name was. I'm getting too old for this stuff. You'd think a woman of her age would be more careful. It's not as if she was a spring chicken, she was definitely on the wrong side of thirty if not nearer forty. She didn't get like that from saying her prayers. And now she's dead outside on the footpath; same thing as happened to Brigid Breslin.'[2] An air embolism had caused their deaths – air entering the bloodstream and causing heart failure. It couldn't have been helped though, she thought, it was an accident and accidents will happen. She had done everything she could. It wasn't her fault that the woman had died. The same procedure had worked perfectly for hundreds of women and was much safer than the method she had used in the 1940s: the insertion of the sea-tangle tent. Her experiences with

Ellen Thompson – for which she had received five years penal servitude in Mountjoy Jail for attempting to procure an abortion back in 1945 – had finished her with the sea-tangle tents. They were just too dangerous. Ellen Thompson had almost died and had of course blurted out everything to the police about Mamie; not about the man who paid for the abortion though – maybe the revenue commissioners would get a kick out of reading his name too.

No, her present method was more successful, though she had lost patients on this one too. But so what? If every doctor in the country was to be held responsible for every patient of his that died then there wouldn't be a doctor or a surgeon left practising. She was bloody good at what she did and that was why they beat a path to her door. She hardly had to advertise anymore, everyone knew her. It wasn't even as if that was the only service she performed: people came to her with dandruff, piles, baldness and, most profitably of all, with constipation, the national obsession of the day. She performed an enema to remember and her return list was substantial. She was a right little cure-all, a one-woman hospital, a healing woman, a kind of white witch like Biddy Early from Clare, who a century earlier had been famous for her cures. Except that Mamie was a fully trained midwife. She had done her training in the National Maternity Hospital in Holles Street in 1925 and was very proud of it. She was a professional and they knew it. She was Nurse Cadden, that's what they called her and that's why they wanted to destroy her: jealousy and spite.

She thought back to her Rathmines days and the hostility

she'd faced because she drove a red MG sportscar and they didn't have the arse in their britches. She still missed that sportscar. It was the sexiest car in the Free State: KG 1647, she remembered it well. It had been imported from Wales. The looks of envy when she whizzed around town in it had to be seen to be believed. Once a man spat in her face! But there was lust in the eyes of the men too; she remembered that as well. It was odd, she didn't really miss her big house, St Maelruin's on the Lower Rathmines Road, but the car, the car! All the men thought that women should be scrubbing and cooking in the kitchen, having a baby each year until they died of thrombosis or high blood pressure. She remembered what she had heard back in Mayo about the place of women in society: 'Keep them barefoot and pregnant,' the boy had said as the others roared with laughter, a laughter that was serious as well as funny. Well, that was not for Mamie Cadden, she would fight them all, as she had all her life.

They could prove nothing anyway. There was no evidence that Helen O'Reilly was ever there. And how would they believe that a woman of Mamie's years could drag the body of a pregnant woman out of her first-floor flat, down the stairs and up the street? After all, she would be sixty-five this year, not that she'd admit that to them. Then there was her arthritis. No, not even a Dublin judge and jury could be so stupid as to think that she could do a thing like that on her own! Not to talk of the commotion she would make dragging a body down the stairs. It would have awoken the whole street not alone the whole house.

Thank God for Standish O'Grady! He hadn't let her

down in her hour of need. He had come over when she called
the night before and had advised her well: 'Cover your
tracks. They have nothing to link you to her.'³ The old saying
was true: A friend in need is a friend indeed! If it weren't for
him she would have no one. Her family was useless. Her
three sisters, Ellie, Teresa and Eliza were all dead – not that
they had been of much use anyway even though she had
given one of them good work in the nursing-home in Rathmines. Her brother, Joe, had let her down back in 1938. She
had wanted him to post bail for her and, though he had
agreed, he hadn't turned up when she was remanded in custody along with her maid, poor, loyal, stupid, Molly O'Grady.
Molly hadn't even been with her on the night in question.
She had told the revenue commissioners about this too. Joe
came in the end but he shouldn't have left them for all that
time in that hellhole of a Mountjoy Jail. She blamed his wife,
a national-school teacher with notions, totally under the
thumb of the priests, and he without the backbone to stand
up to her. They were trying to be respectable and would drop
family for that. The only one of them with any backbone or
loyalty was her cousin, Paddy Cadden, a carpenter who lived
in Dublin. Blast them, she would take on all comers, she was
not broken yet. Why had her father taken them away from
the States back to this bloody godforsaken country? 'I'd have
been a great success in America,' she thought. 'With my
business acumen I'd be a millionairess by now. I'm still an
American citizen. They can't take that away from me.'

The door of her flat was left ajar to see if she could hear
anything from the street. She'd already been outside the front

door looking at the crowd gathering. Two policemen had called earlier and she had taken them up to her room. She told them she had heard nothing during the night and that she had left the radio on, as she couldn't sleep. She'd shown them her bandaged legs. When they'd told her about the woman's body she had said, 'God bless us. Sure it must have been a man that did that.' That might put them off the track – or maybe she should have kept her big mouth shut. They were gone now but would be back again, she could be sure of that. They had persecuted her all her life, even before they had charged her with abandoning that child back in 1938, spreading rumours about bodies of seventeen babies being found in the garden of her house at 183 Lower Rathmines Road. Lies, damn lies and the gardaí had done nothing to scotch them though they knew the truth.

But now she was ready for them. There was nothing in the flat to connect her to Helen O'Reilly lying cold on the street outside. The reporters would be around too. She was looking forward to that. She liked them, at least you could have a bit of a laugh with them – not like the gardaí. She'd tell them about the time she landed a bucket of shite on top of Detective Tom Cryan. She'd given a man an enema that day and had a bucket of shite – enough to cover four acres – in the flat. Cryan and another guard had been following her around for days and as they stood on the street outside she emptied the contents of the bucket right on top of them out through the front window. They didn't know what had hit them and she'd laughed for a week.[4]

Just then there was a light tap on the door. It was John

Moran who lived upstairs with his mother. He was an unemployed baker and was friendly with Mamie. Decent working people with no airs and graces, she thought.

'The gardaí are all over the place,' John spurted out. 'They've found the body of a young woman outside Number 15. They think she's been murdered. I want to ring my girlfriend to tell her. She was here with me last night.'

'I know,' said Mamie. 'I saw you both on the stairs. Who was the young woman, do they know?'

'They do,' John replied. 'They have her bank book. Her name is Helen O'Reilly. Can I use your phone to ring Lizzie?'

'Tear away,' said Mamie, easing herself into her chair so she could listen in on John's conversation with his girlfriend, Elizabeth Burke:

'Pat Rigney, the milkman from Lucan Dairies, was making deliveries to the street when he found the body at about half-six this morning. He was coming into Hume Street from Stephen's Green when he saw what he thought was a bundle of clothes down the street. When he went down the street past the bundle he saw a leg sticking out from it. He went up to it and found that it was the body of a woman. He went round the corner and told a guard he met there.'

When he had finished giving his spectacular news to his girlfriend, he related it again to Mamie. She resumed her breakfast. 'The poor bitch', was all she said as she buttered another slice of bread.[5]

2

Mayo, God Help Us!

It had all started so hopefully. There was love and romance, travel and even a bit of money in Mamie's background, which set her and her family apart in Ireland of the 1890s. Patrick Caden had emigrated to America where he had met Mary McLoughlin of Teirnard in County Mayo (about ten miles from where Pat himself hailed). Teirnard was a rugged, lonely place, which couldn't have been more different from the teeming city of Scranton in Pennsylvania. They were married in 1891; Pat was twenty-seven years of age and his wife was a year older. He worked as a miner in this town that was at the forefront of the American industrial boom, whose fortunes depended solely on the coal-mining industry. Though it was 134 miles from New York City it attracted the immigrant Irish in their thousands with its promise of relatively well-paid work in the mines. The wages were low by American standards but to the poor immigrant Irish they were a godsend.

The young couple settled down in New Street in this rapidly expanding city and Pat went down the mines each day to earn his living. Their firstborn child was a healthy, fair-haired girl and both parents, particularly Pat, doted on her. She was born on 27 October 1891 and christened Mary Anne, soon becoming known only by her pet name of

Mamie.[6] She was baptised in St Peter's Cathedral in Wyoming Avenue by Fr Mangan on 15 November. Pat's brother, Michael, and his wife, Bridget, acted as godparents at the ceremony. Another girl, Ellen, was born in August 1893 but she was not to survive childhood; they later gave the same name to a child born in 1899.

The young Caden family seemed set for the tough challenge which so many of the Irish in America faced at the end of the nineteenth century and which some, like the Kennedys, did with spectacular success. But their future was not to be an American one. Scranton was a hard, ugly place and the loss of their daughter, Ellen, hit them hard. When Pat's father died in 1895 they were only too happy to return to Ireland and the family farm, far from the hustle and bustle of the city and coal-mining life.

The Ireland they found on their return was one which was changing rapidly. Charles Stewart Parnell, the great leader, had died, broken and defeated in Brighton in 1891 in the arms of his beloved wife, Kitty O'Shea. The land agitator, Michael Davitt, from Straide, was elected MP for South Mayo the year the Caden family returned to Ireland, though his great days as Land League leader were winding down. Still, the work of the league in bringing about land reform was proceeding apace. Now tenants could buy their own farms with government assistance – a revolutionary change in rural Ireland.

Pat Caden and his young wife and child were beneficiaries of all this when in 1911 they were able to purchase the Caden family smallholding, becoming owner-occupiers rather than tenants living at the whim of the landlord and his agent.[7] Rents were low and security of tenure had been established. Their house was the largest of the twenty in the townland of Doonbredia, boasting five rooms, which Pat later extended to six. With their American savings they opened a grocery shop in part of the house and built an extra outhouse which gave them a stable as well as a fowl house and a cowhouse. In 1901, they even had a domestic servant, sixteen-year-old Katie Donoghoe.[8]

They had seven children in all, of whom two did not survive infancy. Besides Mamie there was Michael Joseph, their only son whom they called Joe, born in 1897; Ellie, born two years later; Teresa, born in 1900; and Eliza, born in 1906. The new century saw the Caden family settle down to a life not untypical of the better-off small farmer in early twentieth-century Ireland but with a relatively small family by contemporary standards. They would have been termed a 'respectable' family, a step down from 'strong' farmers but way above the landless labourers in the social scale. They were the peculiar product of their times: the new Catholic lower-middle-class, literate and property owning. But things could not have been easy: it was a poor place, the land was poor, and their holding was remote. In 1897, famine stalked north Mayo but they survived; many not so far away from Doonbredia didn't. 'When we survived that we will survive anything,' Pat Caden used to say.

With five women in the house the servant was soon let go. The family all attended school and all except their mother, Mary, could eventually read and write. They were a proud family and their mother's illiteracy was carefully kept from the census takers.[9] The whole family, we are told, was proficient in Irish as well as in English. Mamie never forgot her Irish and was still able to converse in it fifty years later.

The family were Roman Catholics, as were all of their neighbours in the townland. Later on in life Mamie was to become stridently anti-clerical and renounce her Catholicism. In her letter to the revenue commissioners (written the day before Helen O'Reilly's death in 1956) she vehemently denounced two priests: Fr Michael Boylan, the parish priest of St Columba's, Iona Road, on Dublin's northside, and Fr Cathal McCarthy, of Holy Cross College, Clonliffe Road. But it was a dangerous business to take on the priests in 1950s Ireland and Mamie Cadden would pay the price. She did not live by the dictum of Oscar Wilde: 'A man cannot be too careful in the choice of his enemies.' At the end of her 1956 trial, in spite of her background and the dominance of Catholicism in the state, she was to announce defiantly: 'I am not a Catholic.'

Pat Caden spelled his name using only one 'd' – as his beautiful copperplate signature testifies – except in America where the double 'd' was used. His eldest daughter, when she moved to Dublin, was to change her spelling of the name to the more widely used 'Cadden'. Changes in spelling surnames were not infrequent in Ireland then as the final Anglicised version of previously Gaelic names was still undecided. And her name wasn't all she changed! All through her life she seemed to have a charming and amusing inability to tell her real age! Even at the age of sixty-four she declared herself as aged fifty-two years to the authorities in Mountjoy Jail who duly recorded it as such! In 1939 on a similar report she admitted to being thirty-four instead of her forty-seven years!

Mamie, like the others in her family, attended the local national school at Lahardane, the nearest village, about two miles from their house. As a bright and studious girl she stayed on as long as she could swallowing up what learning the small school could give her. She did not leave until she was fifteen. She was remembered as being highly strung and strong-willed, and of not getting on with her family. In reality she was in the same situation as all the women of her generation: a second-class citizen in a man's world. Though the eldest of her family there was no chance that she would inherit the farm or shop which would go to the only boy in the house, Joe. But Mamie, as she soon became known, was not a woman to take second place lightly.

In 1911, the Caden family bought their small farm through the Land Commission from their landlord, the Right Honourable Arthur Jocelyn Charles Gore, the Earl of Arran. The Gores had as recently as the 1880s owned 30,000 acres in Mayo and another 7,000 in Donegal. Pat Caden took ownership of most of it but remarkably about one-and-a-half acres was purchased in Mamie's name. It wasn't a significant portion but was big enough for a small dowry or perhaps a start in life away from Mayo. It made her one of the very few women in the whole country who had land handed over to them during this period. In spite of this, so long as she remained at home, there was nothing for her except a subsidiary role as helper and assistant. The only escape was marriage.

And so she carried on, helping in the shop, helping with the younger children, biding her time until her brother, Joe, grew up and took over. But what was to become of her then? He would get married and Mamie would become the older unmarried sister burden. No wonder she fought with her family. It was a highly frustrating situation for an intelligent and able woman and one she shared with so many others of her generation. For her though it was particularly vexing: she had been born in 'America of the Opportunities' and transported back to Mayo where even contact with other humans was rare, where the drudgery of family duties and services was carried on day in, day out and all for what? For the benefit of her brother, Joe, who would inherit everything while she would be left as the old maid watching while his family grew up around her. And yet she stayed there right through her teenage years, her twenties and into her thirties, probably held there by the fact that she owned a small part of the land and by her love for her father.

As the eldest in the family she soon took on the responsibility of running the shop but there was no future for her there and she knew it. In 1925, her younger sister, Teresa, died of TB and asthma; it was a slow, painful and humiliating death. She had always been delicate and had been very sick for the nine months before her death at just twenty-five years of age. She had worked most of her life in the shop with Mamie but had to be taken out of it long before her death. Customers were hardly likely to buy from a TB patient and the terror of infection could have ruined the business. Teresa's death seems to have galvanised Mamie into taking some action about her own future. She was now going on thirty-four years of age and she knew that if she hung around any longer she might never get out.

One job that Mamie had always fancied was nursing, and especially midwifery: she was fascinated by its skill and importance. Around Doonbredia, the local midwife was the only medical practitioner the local people used with any regularity. Trips to the doctor were rare and expensive but the local midwife was accessible, highly respected and present at all the births. And midwifery was a highly desirable qualification; it had a much higher status in the first half of the century than in the second. So it was agreed with her father that Mamie would go to Dublin to train as a midwife and it would all be paid for by the sale of her small bit of land to him. She had done her duty by her family and now this was to be a sort of a pay-off. The money from the sale would set her up in Dublin, getting her away from Mayo and the homestead – a prospect not unwelcome to her brother Joe who could well imagine the fireworks between any wife he might bring into the household and the hot-headed Mamie.

So in early 1925 Mamie applied to the National Maternity Hospital in Dublin – known then as now as Holles Street – for entry into their six-month midwifery course. Still spelling her name in the style used by her father – with one 'd' – she was accepted. She put down her address as 'Lahardane', the nearest village, transforming herself into a 'townie'; she was not going to be seen as a country bumpkin by the other women or the tutors she would meet!

The course was to run from May to November 1925 and

Mamie lodged in the hospital. She paid her fees of £25 in two instalments in May and September.[10] It was a substantial amount of money – roughly equivalent in value to €1,300 in 2004 – and clearly reflected the high status of the course.[11] Though in her early thirties it must have been a huge feeling of liberation for her, at long last free to pursue her own life. Other women might have found the whole thing hugely intimidating but not Mamie.

The course was certified by the Central Midwifery Board and was for those with no other nursing qualification. But Mamie had been away from education for a long time and found the course difficult and demanding. She failed her exams on two occasions and it was not until 10 December 1926 that she was finally put on the register of midwives. Still, she now had her professional qualification in the profession she had sought: Mamie Cadden had arrived! To indicate her new status she added an extra 'd' to her name!

She set about finding a job immediately. With her qualifications, managerial ability and strong personality she was a great catch for any maternity nursing-home owner. At that time Dublin had up to fifty such institutions, primarily maternity homes, and as many as 200 midwives; they served a huge proportion of the child-bearing women of the city. Each was privately owned and as such challenged the religious orders who were setting up monopolies in the area of medical care with the active collusion of the new politicians who had recently taken over the country. It was a struggle that was to have dire consequences for Mamie, as she was soon to epitomise the independent-minded nursing-home and midwifery sector. The nursing-homes would have had a far more liberal and woman-centred ethos than the religious hospitals.

Mamie found work in the Alverno nursing-home in Dublin's Portland Row in 1927 where the matron was a Mrs McGreal. It was a long way – literally and socially – from her small shop at the foot of Doonbredia Mountain! Back in Doonbredia her brother, Joe, married the local teacher from Lahardane national-school on 18 July 1928. It was a very respectable match: Katie Kavanagh was herself a farmer's daughter from near Boyle in County Roscommon. They were married in St Muiredeach's Cathedral in Ballina with Fr Lavelle officiating. It was a 1920s setpiece of rural social mobility and the young couple would only have to wait three years before extending their smallholding.

The 1920s was a prosperous time in a country quickly recovering from civil war. The Free State, as the new twenty-six-county country was known, was even starting its own state-owned electricity generation and, most modern of all, its own national airline! There was widespread economic optimism as people looked forward to a brighter future.

But then in 1929 came the Wall Street Crash, followed by a world slump. Ireland fell victim to the Great Depression and the loss of prosperity from 1930 on plunged the country into what was in effect a thirty-year recession. This was disastrous enough but it happened side by side with the advent of a deeply conservative state. De Valera was to be the dominant political personality for the next thirty years, while on the clerical front, the austere and reactionary Archbishop of Dublin John Charles McQuaid dominated. What followed for women was a constant undermining of their status and their civil rights. Contraception was banned, as was even its mention. Large families were held up as desirable, patriotic, even godly. Restrictions were set in place to remove married women from the workforce in the public sector, the theory being that this would create more opportunities for the breadwinners, i.e. the men. This so-called 'marriage-ban' soon spilled over into the private sector. It became clear that the only time that women were to be allowed work outside the home was in that short period between adulthood and marriage, or so the authorities wished. But the 1920s and 1930s generation of women did not lie down and accept these restrictions in the way the next generation would. After all this generation had been brought up under a more liberal regime where they had been empowered with certain civil and employment rights by the British administration.

In the new atmosphere dreadful solutions to the problems of fertility and family numbers were sought and the papers reported increased cases of infanticide and child abandonment. In 1929, the *Cork Examiner* reported the extraordinary comments of the trial judge in a case of the concealment of a birth. Judge Kenny said that the number of newly-born infants in the country who were murdered by their mothers at present surpassed belief, that only one out of fifty came up in the courts but that there was a wholesale slaughter of these innocents going on through the country. The official response was to hand these problems over to the police and to the judiciary who would treat them as issues of criminal law rather than social problems. This was the culture into which Mamie Cadden plunged herself with such relish in 1927.

Mamie soon established a good reputation for herself in her new position of midwife. It was a remarkable and rapid transformation from country shopgirl to urban business-woman. She thrived in her new role and in 1929 was able to branch out on her own. Rightly assessing the market require-ment of healthcare for women she went into business for herself and opened a nursing-home at 61 Lower Beechwood Avenue in the Dublin suburb of Ranelagh. It was a modest enough building, a standard two-storey Victorian house on a road that was becoming the centre of Dublin's flat-land. It was here that the real story of 'Nurse Cadden' began.

3

St Maelruin Days

The nursing-home at Beechwood Avenue in Ranelagh was booming as the 1920s turned into the 1930s but Mamie had no intention of settling. The house was too small to allow her business to expand so she found a larger premises on Rathmines Road and set about acquiring it. It was a three-storey-over-basement house with a garage and garden at the back. The purchase of such a premises for a person just arrived into the wage force was a major achievement. She approached the Irish Civil Service and Permanent Building Society of 24 Middle Abbey Street and secured a mortgage from them.[12] This seems to have been the beginning of her relationship with Charles Boyle, a solicitor based at 68 Middle Abbey Street, who acted for her in this transaction.

The transaction was registered on 30 June 1931 and Mamie became the proud owner of one of Dublin's most extensive nursing-homes, prominently placed on the Lower Rathmines Road. At first she called it 4 Ormonde Terrace – as the original group of five attached houses had been grandly called – but she soon returned it to its more accessible address of 183 Lower Rathmines Road. She christened her new premises St Maelruin's after the saint whose feastday, 6 July, coincided with her start of business in 1931. St Maelruin was the founder of the monastery in the then Dublin village of Tallaght and was one of the reformers of the early Irish Church. His feastday was celebrated with wild dancing and all-night drinking until it was abolished by the Dominicans in 1856.

Business at St Maelruin's was brisk from the beginning; Mamie had already built up a clientele and a reputation from her previous position in the Alverno nursing-home and her own nursing-home in Ranelagh. But St Maelruin's was an altogether different venture. It was on a much grander scale and, as it was on one of the capital's major thoroughfares, it was much more visible. Besides the conventional 'lying-in' services – including care during labour and delivery, offered to expectant mothers by Mamie as a midwife – extra services were also available.

Even since her early days in Portland Row Mamie had collaborated with Kathleen McLoughlin who lived at 30 Berkeley Road in the Dublin suburb of Phibsborough. Mc-Loughlin, who described herself as a social worker, performed quite a different job to what we would now expect from a social worker.[13] In an age when the supply of unwanted babies far exceeded the demand for adoptions, McLoughlin, for a fee, would farm out babies to women who would rear them, also for a fee. It was a precursor to the modern system of fostering and was perfectly legal. An unwanted infant would be born in St Maelruin's (perhaps the mother was unmarried or already felt she had as many children as she could cope with) and Nurse Cadden would take responsibility for the child for an 'adoption' fee. Usually the fee was £50, quite a considerable sum but obviously an amount her clients were only too happy to part with for the service. Then Nurse Cadden would contact McLoughlin who would place the babies with mothers who often had children of their own and for whom the extra monthly payment handed over by McLoughlin would be a welcome addition to the household income. McLoughlin would claim, for example, that Nurse Cadden gave her £30 for placing baby X with Mrs X, and would pay Mrs X 30 shillings a month (there were 20 shillings in one pound). McLoughlin had been involved in this type of work since 1912.

All the children placed by her were registered under the Children's Act. The whole process may seem strange now, almost a hundred years later, but it had its advantages over the mass institutionalisation of children which was to replace it. The children were placed in families where it seems they grew up with a full sense of belonging. That they were safer from abuse and exploitation in these families than in the orphanages and reform schools where later generations of them would be sent is also a fact that began to emerge in the closing years of the twentieth century. But the system had its murky side too. It depended on the transfer of the money from the parents to Nurse Cadden, who took her share, to McLoughlin, who also took her share. The foster parents were dependent on McLoughlin for supervision and support as well as the modest payment she gave them and neglect is likely to have occurred.

This system led to Mamie Cadden's nursing-home having a fair share of unmarried mothers among its clientele as Mamie was non-judgemental about the wishes of her patients. But the fostering service was not cheap and was certainly out of reach of working-class or unemployed girls unless paid for by a better-off relative or the child's father. In Dublin of the 1930s, £50 was equivalent to something over €3,000. It was a substantial amount but obviously considered well worth it by the women involved.

However these were not the only activities associated with St Maelruin's. Not all expectant mothers wished to complete their pregnancies and traditional Dublin methods of procuring a miscarriage often led to their confinement in St Maelruin's where the same matter of fact approach to their condition was exercised by Nurse Cadden.

Margaret Berkery, a widow from the Howth Road, tells in a statement to the police that she was so desperate on discovering her pregnancy that she went to London where she purchased liquid Ergot, commonly used as an abortifacient.[14] Ergot preparations were usually administered to stimulate contraction of the womb and so prevent excessive bleeding after childbirth or abortion; when taken during pregnancy it could cause abortion. When the Ergot didn't work she tried to book herself into Nurse Cadden's establishment on the evening of 24 February 1938. However, Mamie had other priorities for that night: she was going to a dance and refused to take Berkery in! Berkery had to wait until the following day, by which time she was bleeding so much that Mamie had to call Dr Percy Seager of 35 Upper Fitzwilliam Street to attend. The baby was born dead – no doubt because of the Ergot ingestion – and was buried in the back garden. Dr Seager subsequently denied carrying out any 'operations' in the nursing-home.

The finding of the remains of this baby in the garden of the nursing-home in 1938 was to lead to one of the enduring urban myths about Mamie Cadden: namely that the remains of between fourteen and seventeen infants were found buried in her garden.[15] In fact there was just one, that delivered of Mrs Berkery. It was a very damaging rumour though and one that was to follow Nurse Cadden beyond the grave and into the current urban mythology of Dublin. Mamie was totally unrepentant: 'You cannot say that was a child,' she said when confronted by the gardaí with the find, 'it was a foetus.'

The gardaí were already frequent visitors to the home and their adverse relationship with Mamie was brewing. One of her patients at the end of 1936 was a sergeant's wife who seems to have been the mother of a boy fostered out in that year. This fact was thrown in the face of the gardaí by Mamie during each of their many rows.

As the 1930s rolled by Mamie was on top of the world. Her balance at the National Bank, a few doors up from St Maelruin's, was healthy, though never brimming over. In 1936 she re-mortgaged St Maelruin's but always kept out of debt in spite of a fairly fast lifestyle. Women were coming from all over the country, even from across the border, to avail of the services in St Maelruin's, so much so that she now had a staff to assist her: according to the inspector of nursing-homes she employed her own sister as a nurse; her cousin, Mary O'Grady (who was referred to as Molly), a brunette with a sallow complexion and about thirty-four years old in 1938, was her constant companion and was employed as a maid. She had followed Mamie from Alverno to Beechwood Avenue and finally into Rathmines and had known her before she left Mayo. Molly hailed from Newfield, Rosturk, not far from Mamie's old home. Though she had no medical training Mamie was to describe her as being 'better than a nurse'. Dr Percy Seager of 35 Upper Fitzwilliam Street was the doctor who attended the nursing-home and she also often engaged the professional services of Mr Lavelle the dentist.

Mamie was right at the centre of whatever Bohemian life there was in Dublin in the 1930s. She befriended college students and was a jovial supplier of alcohol and entertainment to them. She claimed later on that she was friendly with Edward Preston Ball, a member of the small gay society of the Dublin of his day that included the famous Gate Theatre actors and lovers Hilton Edwards and Micheál Mac Liammóir. Ball was convicted in 1936 of murdering his mother, Lavinia, because she wouldn't finance him on a tour to Egypt with the Gate Theatre. Mrs Ball had been married but was separated from her husband, the distinguished doctor, Charles Preston Ball, who practised at Pembroke Road in Ballsbridge. Her body was never found but her bloodstained Austin 7 car was recovered in Corbawn Lane, near the sea, in the suburb of Shankill. A suitcase full of bloodstained clothes, which Ball had left at the flat of his boyfriend, Charles Monson, helped to incriminate him. It was a major and notorious crime of its day.

Ball, who was just turning twenty at the time, was found guilty but insane. He was incarcerated in the Dundrum Criminal Lunatic Asylum from which he was released in 1950. Mamie was always loyal to her friends and would never admit to Edward's guilt. To the end of her days she would say referring to Ball and his father: 'It was the oul fella that done it but he had to take the rap.'[16] She insisted that Edward was with her in her car on the night of the murder though this was not mentioned during his trial.

Her great status symbol was her car, a red open-top MG sportscar manufactured in 1932 and first registered to Mamie on 4 April 1934. It had been imported from Cardiff. Soon she was a regular sight in Dublin, whizzing through its streets with her blonde hair blowing in the breeze. It was, to say the least, incongruous in the economically depressed Free State, where austerity was promoted by the de Valera-led government. Ireland was in the throes of an economic war with Britain and unemployment and emigration were on the increase. It's easy to imagine that Mamie provoked massive envy and resentment. It was bad enough flaunting her exotic possessions but the fact that she was a woman made her audacity even greater.

There was no legalised form of adoption in the new state and the Catholic Church was highly suspicious of the idea. Legislation on adoption was not introduced until 1952 and then only after it had been closely vetted by Archbishop McQuaid. Babies were handed out almost on request to childless couples who were trusted by the authorities. In such an informal system abuses were bound to occur especially as the state paid a fee to the carers of parentless children. A racket had been in existence all through the 1930s. A number of babies were being abandoned on roadside spots in Dublin and the surrounding counties where they would be found before any serious damage to their health could occur from exposure. The babies would be well wrapped up in good quality clothes and were not the usual newborn babes abandoned by young frightened girls. To the gardaí this seemed much more organised.

The highly visible and mobile Mamie Cadden was their chief suspect, not only of abandoning babies but also of facilitating abortions in her nursing-home. There seemed to be a total lack of sympathy between the authorities and the nursing-home. However, they were unable to find any evidence to support the abortion theory. When Superintendent Hughes accused a patient in the home of having had an abortion he was rounded on by Mamie: 'A superintendent had the cheek to accuse a girl from Clare of murdering her own baby when in fact the girl had given birth to a monster that had to be destroyed.'[17] Against such aggressive defence of her business and patients the gardaí just couldn't move – ironically as events transpired the gardaí turned out to be very frequent users of the facilities provided by Mamie.

There was also the fact that Mamie's nursing-home was very professionally run. Emily Mary Brady, the inspector of midwives from Dublin corporation, reported that in the ten years between 1928 and 1938 she had visited Nurse Cadden's homes and 'never found anything wrong'. She frequently inspected the rooms and the instruments. In 1936 she visited the home in Rathmines on four occasions and in 1937 on five occasions. Dr Russell, the registrar of births at Dublin Castle, also visited St Maelruin's. As far as Dublin corporation, which was the regulatory body for nursing-homes in its area, was concerned, St Maelruin's was being properly run.

In 1935, the status of women in the Irish Free State suffered a major setback with the new Criminal Law Amendment Act, an act that would deliver Ireland from any trace of sexual liberalism inherited from the old regime. The bill was the result of the deliberations of an all-party committee and dealt with many aspects of sexuality including prostitution and brothel-keeping. However, it was Section 17 that was to have a wide-reaching effect on the future of Irish women. It forbade the sale, advertising and the importation for sale of contraceptives. The bill had only one opponent: Dr Robert Rowlette, the Independent TD for Trinity College. He was a professor in Trinity and a former British army soldier in the Medical Corps. Dr Rowlette contended that the ban on the sale of contraceptives would lead to an increase in infanticide and criminal abortion.[18] How right he proved to be.

It was a dark time for Irish women who wished to control their own fertility, and it lasted until 1962 when the birth-control pill finally became available in the country.[19]

Desperate times provoked desperate remedies. Without information on fertility control the measures resorted to by women ranged from the ludicrous to the pathetic. Efforts to induce a miscarriage were usually attempted by bringing on some sort of physical trauma. Dublin folklore tells us that women at certain stages in pregnancy would jump off their gas cookers! Attempts at contraception were probably even less scientific. One doctor relates how he delivered a baby with the top of a Guinness bottle on its head. The mother had hoped that this would act as a contraceptive.[20]

The bill of course was accompanied by a garda crackdown on abortion services. There were eleven prosecutions or investigations. Mamie Cadden's establishment in Rathmines was one of the places investigated but the gardaí could find no evidence against her. But Ireland was changing. It was drifting slowly but surely towards becoming a state in which Catholic social policy was the law of the land. This would finally become a reality when the new constitution came into force on 1 January 1938 and the 'special position of the Catholic Church' was recognised.

4

The Majesty of the Law

1938 was to be the *annus horribilis* for Mamie. Business was good. She was at the height of her powers: physically, mentally, socially and financially; a successful businesswoman, a medical professional and certainly a glamorous character about town in the dimming lights of Dublin city. She was forty-seven years old, a fact belied by her mass of blonde hair which was her pride and joy and shown at its best as she darted about in her red sportscar. Molly O'Grady was her usual companion as she drove extensively around the city and adjoining counties. She went to dances, dined frequently in the Gresham and drank in the Shelbourne. It seemed as if she were making up time for her lost years working in the shop in Mayo.

In early June 1938, the country was in the throes of a general election campaign. The minority Fianna Fáil government that ruled with just an even half of the Dáil seats now struck out for an overall majority. The government was buoyed by the Anglo-Irish Agreement which had ended the economically ruinous tariff struggle between the Free State and Great Britain: the 'Economic War'; and which saw the handing over of the 'Treaty Ports'. It seemed to many that the prosperity of the pre-Wall Street Crash days might return. Polling day was to be Friday, 17 June 1938.

On Tuesday 14 June Mamie Cadden drove from her home in Rathmines into County Meath. At least one passenger and probably a second accompanied Mamie. From events that were to occur later it is now safe to assume that the second passenger was a two-and-a-half-month-old infant, the daughter of a 'merchant' from the small town of Prosperous in County Kildare. The baby had been born in Nurse Cadden's nursing-home in Rathmines on 31 March.[21] The parents had paid £50 as an adoption fee to Nurse Cadden.

It was a warm summer night and many of the locals were out and about on the road between Dunshaughlin and Navan: some off to visit their neighbours, relatives and friends; some just taking the air; and others lounging around at the crossroads. All noticed when a red car roared past: Mamie was having some trouble with her exhaust, which added even further to the noise of her car. James Stoney, who lived in a roadside cottage on the other side of Dunshaughlin, saw the red sportscar on his way to visit his son. It must have been somewhat conspicuous on this country road where any motor vehicle was notable, especially as the day drew to a close.

As Stoney returned home on foot at about 9.45 p.m. he was again passed by the sportscar and he again noticed the two women in it. As he drew near Doran's cottage he heard a baby cry and, continuing around the corner, he was shocked to find a well wrapped-up child lying in the grass margin. Amazingly he left the baby where it was and returned to the nearby cottage where Agnes Doran was standing at her gate. He told her what he had seen. She claimed afterwards that she had heard a car stopping, presumably to drop off the baby. They were both just around a bend on the road and though they could hear they could not see the baby. Surprisingly she too left the baby where it was and Stoney headed back into Dunshaughlin to report the incident to the gardaí. There he met Sergeant Robert Gough who drove Stoney back to the place where the baby lay undisturbed.

The kind-hearted sergeant took the shivering baby in his arms and in his own words, she was 'cold and trembling'. He took her back to Dunshaughlin where his wife took care of her. Later on that evening the little girl was taken to the county hospital in Navan. She wore a white vest, a cream coloured frock, coat and jacket, all covered by a white shawl and she seemed to have suffered no lasting ill effects from her ordeal.

The next day Sergeant Gough spent some time taking statements from the many people who had been on the road that night; in an era before television, walking the roads in the evening was a popular social activity. All had seen the red sportscar drive in towards Navan before 10 p.m. and return a short time later. (Witnesses were a little vague about times, few perhaps owning watches.) Three of those interviewed had previously seen this spectacular vehicle driven by a lady during trips they had taken to Dublin: such was Nurse Cadden's visibility! All reported that there were two women in the car.

Thomas Anderson had seen the car in Dunshaughlin with two women in it. He had earlier passed the spot where the baby was found and testified that there was nothing there at 9 p.m. Nellie Killoran saw the car twice on the road and calculated that because of the interval between sightings that it had travelled on to Navan but no further. James Doran saw the two women as well and remembered that one wore a black fur coat. Then there were the boys standing at the cross. The boys, Francis Waters, Reg Fleming, Pat McCormack, James McGuinness and James Lanney, were given a rare thrill when the red sportscar passed containing two glamorous women.

On Thursday Sergeant Gough visited the detective branch in Dublin Castle. From here it seemed no problem identifying the red sportscar especially one driven by 'a fair haired woman'. In the company of Detective Michael Neill from Dublin Castle he headed out to Rathmines to pay a visit to Nurse Cadden. They stood for a while across the road looking over at the house and were in luck: there was Mamie herself supervising a workman who was doing some minor repairs to the front door. Detective Neill knew Mamie by sight and when she went back into the house they went up the steps and knocked on the door. They were answered by a dark-haired woman in her thirties whom neither of them knew at the time. She told them she was Mary McCann, that she had only recently come to work in St Maelruin's and that Nurse Cadden, whom she called Miss McCadden, wasn't in. The pair informed 'Mary' that they had just seen Mamie outside the house and the poor maid who was, of course, Molly O'Grady, had to go and get her, pretending unconvincingly that she had just come in. But if Molly was intimidated then Mamie was a tower of strength.

'Yes, as a matter of fact I was in Navan on Tuesday night,' she told the gardaí. 'I was with a boy whose name I do not care to mention.'

She told them that she had got lost and ended up in Duleek and so did not pass the roadside where the child had been abandoned.

When asked for the nursing-home register that she was obliged by law to keep, Mamie produced it as well as a small red notebook that she kept as a private register. She read the information to the men while sitting on a piano stool in her parlour. It seemed from the official register which was perfectly intact that seven babies had been born in the home since 1 March 1938: six girls and one boy. However only six of them were registered with Dr Russell, the city medical officer in Dublin Castle. One baby girl was missing. The gardaí left but the affair was not over by any means. Still Mamie was sure that there were no witnesses who had seen the baby being left on the roadside.

The next day was polling day in the general election and Sergeant Gough, in common with many members of the police force, was on duty protecting the ballot outside his local polling station of Dunshaughlin. At 7 p.m. who did he spot heading from the direction of Navan in her red sportscar but Mamie Cadden accompanied by her maid, Molly O'Grady. An hour and a half later on its way back to Dublin he stopped the car and enquired into their business in Meath that night. Mamie cheekily asked of him, 'Do you think I dumped another one this evening?' and roared laughing as she drove into the sunset. Not only was she spotted by the sergeant but she was seen by many of the other witnesses who had been around on the previous Tuesday night: Agnes Doran, the boys at Ross Cross who had assembled again, James Stoney and the ever-present Nellie Killoran. Thomas Anderson on this occasion took the number of the car, KG 1647, as did Thomas Lanney, James Lanney's father.

They were all amazed to see the same car for the second time in just four days in the same general area and even at a similar time. On this occasion they took great care to notice the occupants in detail. All reported seeing two women, one blonde and one brunette. None had taken the registration number on the previous Tuesday night but now they had the opportunity and motive. The abandoned baby in the townland of Rosetown was the talk of the county. The two women in the car were committed to memory. It was all right for Mamie, she never denied her presence in Meath that evening but it was a different matter for Molly O'Grady, guilty or not she was now linked in the visual memory of the witnesses as a passenger in the car and in the company of Mamie Cadden.

But the gardaí still had very little evidence. Nobody had seen the car stop and nobody had seen the baby in the car, but there was a baby found and there was an infant unaccounted for in the St Maelruin record book. It was inevitable that the gardaí would pursue the matter: they had been looking for evidence to connect Mamie with child abandonment and abortion since the early 1930s and this was the closest they'd ever been to nailing her.

On 6 July Mamie phoned the garda station in Rathmines. She wanted to make a statement. Any hopes the gardaí had of a confession were soon to come to nothing. Mamie still claimed that she was innocent and that Molly had not been in the car with her. She now informed the police that she had a witness to back this up. Bridget O'Shaughnessy of 30 Hollybank Road in Drumcondra would make a statement that she called to the nursing-home on the night in question and had tea and a chat with Molly O'Grady. O'Shaughnessy was a typist with Associated Properties of 4 Grafton Street and originally hailed from Tynagh, County Galway. She seemed a reputable sort of witness. Mamie claimed that the 'boy' in the car was a medical student and was afraid that coming forward would damage his future prospects. Furthermore she ludicrously added that her car often stopped when she was going uphill and that was perhaps what Mrs Doran heard when she stated that she had heard a car stopping on the night in question.

On 8 July 1938 the gardaí visited the nursing-home again, a full three weeks after their first visit, with a view to gaining further evidence. This time Detective Cryan and Detective O'Connor accompanied Sergeant Gough.

It was a confrontational visit to put it mildly and again took place in the parlour. Present were Mamie, Molly and the three gardaí. Mamie was in fighting form. The registration book now had loose pages as some of its pages had been removed. It was taken into police custody, as was her private record book. 'The only bastards born in this house,' Mamie roared at them, 'were fathered by guards.' Molly O'Grady was questioned about her identity as she had given the name of Mary McCann on the previous visit. Initially Mamie would not let Molly answer any questions and spoke for her. Detective Tom Cryan asked her to desist to which Mamie replied,

'I am remaining here as a witness. There's three of you to one of her.' Detective Cryan asked her to leave the room, which she eventually did. Still Molly didn't admit to her real identity until she went out and consulted with Mamie. Her lame excuse was that she had heard so many lies that she eventually decided to tell some herself! She made a statement giving her real name and stating that she was from Newfield, Rosturk, County Mayo, and that she had known Mamie before she left Mayo. She further admitted that she was indeed a distant relative of hers. After these revelations Mamie came back into the parlour and quickly leapt to Molly's defence: 'Can't she use any name she likes?' she exclaimed. 'I told her there was no harm in it.'

Whatever her motives Mamie was never afraid to take responsibility for others. Molly was not a nurse, she said, but she was better that any nurse. She knew as she had dealt with seven or eight of them in a single year. Mamie said that Molly had been with her since 1928 [*sic*] in the nursing-home in Beechwood Avenue and had worked in the Three Counties hospital in Bedford with Mamie's sister. She added rather sadly that Molly never went out except with her. Later on she was to claim that she had put Molly up to using the false name though it seems much more likely that it was a spur of the moment decision by the frightened countrywoman when first confronted by the police. It also appears that they started working together in the Alverno nursing-home in Portland Row – Mamie's first place of employment – and not in Beechwood Avenue. Whatever the little lies Mamie told to protect Molly, she seemed genuinely fond of her.

The fact that Mamie thought that all this might get the gardaí to back off showed that she did not appreciate their commitment to pressing charges. On 11 July 1938, less than a month after the incident, the gardaí arrived at 183 Lower Rathmines Road and arrested Mamie and Molly. The shock and humiliation of arrest deeply affected Mamie and she maintained a deep and abiding hatred for Detective Tom Cryan until her dying day, believing that the witch-hunt was all his doing.

The arrest had something of the farce about it: the nursing-home was quite busy and Mamie ushered her clients around the place hoping to avoid contact with the gardaí. Two women were put in the garage with her famous car where Detective Cryan subsequently found them cowering beside the vehicle!

The next day the identification parade was held at the Bridewell police station. In those days witnesses were compelled to attend identification parades in person and had to lay their hands on the persons they identified. To make things even more difficult Mamie had dyed her hair black, not that that was much of a disguise: she was a national figure now, even appearing on the front of the *Daily Mail* slinking sexily in front of her sportscar underneath her crowning glory of black hair![22] The witnesses called were a selection of the characters who were on the road in Meath that night. The boys from the cross were not called but Nellie Killoran, Mr and Mrs Doran, Thomas Anderson and James Stoney were.

Stoney was a key witness as he was the one who found the baby and would have seen the car shortly before, and yet he had a problem at the identification parade. He failed to identify Mamie Cadden and put his hand on the woman standing beside her. There was also a problem about James Doran's identification of Molly O'Grady. He said in evidence that the passenger in the car had a fur coat. Molly wore a fur coat at the identification parade but was not identified by Doran, a situation that the trial judge was to describe as 'strange'. Thomas Anderson also had a problem about identifying O'Grady and would only state that he was 'nearly sure' of her identity.

Though the crime was committed in County Meath the first court appearance on the case took place in Naas, County Kildare, on 13 July 1938. District Justice Reddin presided and seemed astonished at the testimony given by Sergeant Gough, much of which was not backed up by a shred of evidence. Gough was as dramatic and blunt as he was unsupported by facts:

'I am in possession of information,' he said, 'that infants have been found abandoned in various parts of County Dublin and the adjoining counties during the last two or three years and I have good reason for suspecting that those infants or some of them were abandoned by Nurse Mary Anne Cadden and Mary O'Grady.' He never did elaborate on the 'information' or the 'good reason' for these suspicions but his testimony was deeply effective.

'Do you suggest that there is a system of abandoning infants?' asked the shocked district justice.

'We have not yet completed our investigations,' said Detective O'Connor.

The women hadn't a chance of being released for lack of evidence as they had hoped. Worse still it looked as if they were going to be tainted with, if not formally charged with, the abandonment of *all* the children in the Dublin area. They were remanded in custody to the Dunshaughlin Court until 26 July and the grim Mountjoy Jail was to hold them. The humiliation for the proud and haughty Mamie Cadden must have been severe. At the top of the pile a month earlier – the country woman who had made good in the big city, the farmer's daughter from Mayo – she was now a prisoner in Mountjoy. The horror of jail for her poor maid Molly O'Grady too must have been intense.

The search of Mamie's house in Rathmines now began in earnest including the extreme measure of digging up the garden. The day after the court case a parcel was taken away from the scene. There was a full contingent of police present including Detective Superintendent John McGloin, Superintendent W. Cuddihy, Inspector R. Wolfe and, of course, Detectives Cryan and O'Connor. What they found was the remains of an infant girl. When confronted with this Mamie had all the details and the dates ready for them though she was quite reticent as to the identity of the mother. From the details however the gardaí had no difficulty in tracing the unfortunate woman: Margaret Berkery of 201 Howth Road, the widow who had checked into Nurse Cadden's home where she was given medical treatment by Dr Percy Seager which probably saved her life.

Cadden and O'Grady next appeared at Dunshaughlin Court on 26 July 1938, by which time they were national news.

They travelled from Mountjoy to the court in the prison van and a battery of photographers awaited them. The writer for the *Irish Independent* reported that there were 'among the spectators a number of well-dressed women'.[23] The *Evening Mail* used the same leading terms. The implication seems to have been that these were the very type of women who would use such services as supplied by Nurse Cadden, herself a brazen example of 'a well-dressed woman'.

Mamie had lost what little patience she possessed and dismissed Mr Noyk, her solicitor. This was to prove a serious mistake. Michael Noyk was a highly respected Dublin Jewish solicitor and had defended some of the Volunteers during the War of Independence. She replaced him with Charles Boyle who had acted for her when she purchased 183 Lower Rathmines Road. Boyle assured the court that the defence would produce 'a complete answer to the charges'. The barrister for the defence was Joseph A. M. McCarthy. At this stage the gardaí had very little evidence against her. It wasn't even clear exactly what charges were to be preferred. Kevin Haugh took over the case for the state. He was assisted by Thomas Hannan and Ambrose Stern. The case was adjourned until 3 August to Kilmainham Court in Dublin, bail was refused and leave to examine Mamie's bank accounts was given to the gardaí.

There was one further adjournment until the case recommenced at Howth on 10 August they had one of their few breaks when the vacation judge, Mr Justice Gavan Duffy, allowed for bail. They appeared again at Kilmainham Court on 15, 19 and 23 August when statements from witnesses were taken. No bail money had yet arrived much to the frustration of the women. Finally, at the very end of the month, the bail of £300 was put together by her brother, Joe, and William Kavanagh (her sister-in-law's father from Annagh, Ballyfarmon, near Boyle) who had put up £150. Mamie's father had not let her down and had used his influence on behalf of his beloved daughter.

After almost two months of imprisonment Mamie and Molly were free. For Mamie though, her woes were only beginning: her business was in ruins and her reputation was in the gutter. She was now Ireland's most notorious woman, an abandoner of children in whose garden were the remains of several infants – or so the gossips said. She could only look forward to her trial with fear and trepidation.

While they were in custody there were further instances of abandoned babies in the very areas where the gardaí were so sure that Mamie and Molly were the chief perpetrators. On 10 August the *Evening Mail* reported that a baby had been found in the porch of Rathmines Roman Catholic church. Tragically the child died and the city coroner, Dr Brennan, noted that the cause of death was 'lack of skilled attention'. A more horrific case was reported on 10 August against May Sommerville of Knockatuly, Monaghan, who was charged with infanticide. The charge was that she drowned her daughter's baby in a well. On 27 August a week-old baby was found in Burtontown, Balrath, County Meath. Fortunately this baby was quite healthy when discovered. On 31 August Margaret Cullinan of Brooklawn, Donnybrook was charged with abandoning a child on 30 July and was bound over to keep the peace for a year by District Justice Lennon – this was a very lenient treatment especially considering what Mamie and Molly were going through at the time. The case was brought by the same detectives as in the Cadden case: Detectives O'Connor and Cryan.

The time-frame of these cases demonstrates the extent of the problem in Ireland at the time and gives a clear indication that whatever happened in Meath on 14 June 1938 that Mamie Cadden was nothing more than a small part of a major social crisis concerning unwanted pregnancies. One might have expected that these cases would have lessened the pressure on the Cadden case. In fact the case against Mamie would now intensify.

Far from stepping down the investigation, new charges were now brought by the state. Mamie was charged on two counts of demanding money under false pretences. These related to statements made by two women who had their babies in St Maelruin's. One was Annie Hudson, on whose behalf Mamie had received £50 from Annie McDonnell. She had taken the money on the understanding that she would have the baby adopted and cared for by a community of nuns or placed in a Catholic home. This alleged offence happened around 14 March 1938. The other charge related to a child about to be born to Mary Clarke. Mamie got another £50 from Patrick Clarke to have the baby adopted and cared for in an institution set up for that purpose.

The chief state solicitor in a letter to the attorney-general advised that there might 'be difficulty in bringing home to Cadden the two cases – Clarke and Hudson'.[24] But the attorney-general still seemed happy to leave the progress of the case in the hands of the prosecuting barrister, Kevin Haugh, in a strange delegation of responsibility. Haugh decided to proceed with the charges despite the chief state solicitor's concerns.

On 25 September Mamie Cadden was returned to custody and on the following day was charged at the Dublin District Court in front of Senior Justice Little, the judge who had given the initial warrant to Sergeant Gough to arrest the two women. The charges related to Mamie's offer of 'an adoption service' to Clarke and Hudson for £50 when they first came into her home. The allegation was that she was acting as a maternity nurse by putting herself forward as a person qualified to arrange adoptions. When questioned on this she answered quite plainly, 'Isn't that what I am?' After some bitter exchanges between Charles Boyle and the prosecution Mamie was remanded on further bail.

Mamie had lived life in the fast lane since her arrival in Dublin. Even though her business had become a success she was a great consumer and as a consequence was never replete with cash. Now however, with her business effectively closed, she faced a financial crisis. With no income and an expensive legal team she was literally penniless. Her bank accounts show that she emptied her Bank of Ireland current account on 15 July of its last £100 and her thrift account in the National Bank was emptied of its remaining £63 on 29 July. Furthermore there would have been the question of her outstanding re-mortgage repayments from Rathmines Road to the Irish Civil Service and Permanent Building Society. She was in serious trouble indeed.

There was no legal aid available in a case of this nature and Mamie was very demanding as to the quality and effectiveness of her legal representatives. After all, she had already replaced her solicitor, Mr Noyk, with Charles Boyle. Boyle then took the extraordinary step of writing to the attorney-general about this financial situation and his unwillingness to proceed until the money was produced 'up front'. It seemed a very harsh approach. On 20 October 1938 he wrote: 'My clients are on bail and have instructed me to bring in Senior and Junior Counsel on their behalf at the trial. At the time she did so she was perfectly satisfied that she would have no difficulty in providing the sums of money required for her defence, unfortunately the matter has not been so easy as she thought.'[25] Boyle asked the attorney-general for an adjournment so that the money could be secured beforehand.

The matter of an adjournment was ultimately in the hands of the trial judge or the state solicitor for the county in question, in this case Meath. It seems strange that Boyle would bypass both and appeal directly to the attorney-general. He perhaps expected a more favourable response from the attorney-general. His own excuse for not going through the proper channels was that 'time was running out'.

On the following day a letter from the attorney-general's office stated quite clearly 'no resistance will be offered on behalf of the attorney-general to your application if and when it is made to the Circuit Judge'. He couldn't have expected better. Given the speed of the reply one wonders if the attorney-general even consulted the state solicitor on the matter. Charles Boyle was evidently well connected in legal circles and now perhaps he was using his clout to ensure that the case did not progress until Mamie Cadden had produced the money for his and the other members of the legal team's fees.

The implications were drastic for Mamie. Having exhausted her cash resources she now had only her nursing-home and residence, the famous St Maelruin's. She was forced to put it on the market. Her great achievement, the purchase of this extensive property by a former shopgirl from Mayo, now came crashing down about her ears. Nevertheless she knew of no other way to progress. If she won, as she was sure she would, she could start again. After all the gardaí, even after four months of investigation, still only had circumstantial evidence about the baby abandonment in Meath and the other charges were just put in to persecute her. She insisted that the Clarke child was given to the 'social worker', Kathleen McLoughlin, and that the Hudson child was taken away by her mother. They couldn't nail anything on her in these two cases.

The house went on the market in October 1938 and the sale was completed in May 1939. The auctioneer was John Megahy whose business was located near Charles Boyle's on Middle Abbey Street. Boyle acted as solicitor for both Mamie and the purchaser. Dublin was a poorer city at the end of the 1930s and the chances of St Maelrun's remaining in the nursing-home or medical care sector were nil. In fact Francis Vanston of 31 Northumberland Avenue, Dun Laoghaire, purchased the house and turned it into flats.[26]

As the number of nursing-homes run by midwives dwin-
dled in the face of competition from state-backed and religious hospitals Mamie's clients were forced to turn to the
voluntary hospitals. The Catholic institutions were all run
by religious orders where the patients would be treated under
a system of medical ethics far different and less woman-centred than those of Mamie and the other maternity nursing-
homes in Dublin. Whether they acknowledged it or not, the
demise of the private nursing-home sector meant more patients and more control for the religious-run hospitals and
the doctors. It was to become increasingly the norm for pregnant women to go to hospital for the delivery of their babies.

Even the role of midwife, a high status profession in the
first half of the century was now having its independence
undermined. It had existed quite independently from general
nursing and was controlled by its own governing body, the
Central Board of Midwives. Soon it too would come under
attack and the process would end with the Central Board of
Midwives being subsumed into An Bord Altranais (the
Nursing Board). In effect midwifery was to be denied the
high status it had enjoyed for the previous hundred years; it
was to become a mere branch of general nursing.

To round off Mamie's year of disaster came the death of
her beloved father on 13 December.[27] He had suffered dread-
fully from the shame of the charges brought against his fav-
ourite daughter. He had been bursting with pride at her
achievements: her purchase and running of one of Dublin's
biggest nursing-homes, her professional qualifications, her
beautiful motor car, in fact all her badges of material wealth.

His only son Joe had done well, too, marrying the local schoolteacher and greatly increasing the size of his small-holding with the help of the Land Commission, but it was Mamie who had his heart. What a wonderful fairytale come true it had all been – and then in 1938 to hear of the charges of child abandonment and later on those of taking money on false pretences! He had nearly died of the shame. Neighbours could talk of nothing else and he could think of nothing else. His poor little girl Mamie, what would become of her?

Pat Caden was seventy-five when he died, having out-lived his wife Mary. He died of old age and 'congestion of the lungs'. He had been quite ahead of his time signing up his daughter as owner of some land and giving her experience in ownership and in running their small shop which would prove invaluable to her in her business dealings in later life. He was never able to control her wild side or her fiery temper but he loved that part of her too. His death was a shattering blow to her. It came at what was, she thought, her lowest point, before she could beat the charges against her and re-start her business.

5

The Verdict

As 1938 turned into 1939 a dismissal of Mamie's case became more and more unlikely. All the evidence against her was circumstantial with regard to the abandonment charges and the charges of procuring money on false pretences were based on even flimsier evidence. However, to make up for the quality of the case, more quantity was added and Mamie was charged with abandoning those babies for which she had in September been charged with asking for money under false pretences. Everything possible was being done to convict her.

The case was rescheduled for 18 April 1939 with trial judge Mr Justice Black, but it didn't begin until Monday 1 May. Immediately it was big news. The courtroom was packed each day and the proceedings were printed in full by the papers.

The case opened on May Day with the state counsel Kevin Haugh announcing that it was one 'of the greatest importance'. James Stoney gave his evidence of finding the infant on the roadside on that night of 14 June 1938 around the bend of the road from Doran's cottage on the road between Dunshaughlin and Navan. He said when he first heard the baby cry he thought that there might 'be tinkers there'. The five loiterers at Ross Cross described the passing of the red sportscar with the two women in it. They reported seeing it head in the direction of Navan but thought it returned too quickly for it to have reached that town.

On Tuesday, 2 May 1939, Sergeant Robert Gough of Dunshaughlin gave his evidence. He described visiting the scene of the abandonment and taking care of the baby that had seemingly been left untouched since its discovery many hours before. In a damaging statement for the defence he described his visit two days later to the nursing-home in Rathmines and his reception by Molly O'Grady who had tried to conceal her identity from him. He told of meeting the two women the following day outside the polling station in Dunshaughlin when Mamie brazenly asked him: 'Do you think we dropped another one tonight?' He detailed his next visit to the nursing-home in July when the register of births there had two pages missing and when Mamie failed to explain why one of the seven births since 1 March had not been registered with the authorities.

The following day the defence (J. A. McCarthy, Charles Boyle and his son, C. V. Boyle) sought to discredit the garda evidence and to establish the existence of some sort of campaign by the gardaí against Mamie and her nursing-home. Initially it pointed out that garda wives were frequent users of Mamie's services: the first patient there in 1931 was the wife of a sergeant in the gardaí; in 1937 a superintendent's wife attended; and in November that year another garda wife was a patient. What all this was supposed to prove is unclear. It certainly must have annoyed and embarrassed the police force but it was hardly conducive to Mamie's acquittal.

Next came the role of Molly O'Grady in the affair. Mamie,

as the chief defendant, was unequivocal on the matter. The allegation that Molly O'Grady was with her was 'a blasted lie', she said. It is strange that though she never denied her own presence in Meath that night she always vehemently denied the presence of Molly O'Grady. 'It is rather foolish,' she said, 'to think of a girl that never got married in her life to think of abandoning this child.' This intervention on behalf of Molly O'Grady certainly had a strong effect on the jury.

On Thursday 4 May it was time for the defence to address the jury; Mamie's barrister, J. A. McCarthy, did so in full bombastic style. He decried the 'silly-season' publicity that had brought Mamie Cadden such coverage and notoriety. A more serious allegation, though unproven, was the allegation of a concerted garda plot to entrap Mamie. McCarthy criticised the methods of the police and said that one of the officers in the case (presumably Cryan or Neill) had engaged in a policy of encirclement in relation to the defendants. Exaggerating wildly, especially in the case of Mamie, he described the defendants as being 'lonely and unprotected women without a friend in the world'. Sergeant Gough had been overpowered by publicity, he said, and had sought to bring Dunshaughlin 'out of the rut of the unknown'. He was hardly less bombastic about the nursing-home where he said 'children of shame' were born to those who 'fell by the wayside and were entitled to take steps as would prevent or hinder the burden of shame falling on their people at home'. He praised Mamie's qualifications to excess, even stating that she had pursued post-graduate training in the Rotunda

Maternity hospital. (The Rotunda has no record of any such course taken by her, so we can safely assume this was an embellishment.)[28] He did however give a good account of how the extensive press coverage must prejudice the outcome: 'With photographers and pressmen waiting around to blazon them before the world, they had as much chance as a snowball in a certain hot quarter of giving a coherent account of their movements.'

Friday 5 May was the final day of the trial. Mr Justice Black summed up and was clearly unimpressed with the defence. He wondered why Mamie's boyfriend hadn't shown up to verify her story of his presence in the car with her that night. He seemed to be mystified as to how such a person, if he existed, would be so lacking in gallantry as not to turn up to support his girlfriend. Inevitably the conclusion must be that no such person existed. The other missing witness is more mysterious. Mamie had volunteered in the second statement she made to the police that Bridget O'Shaughnessy of 30 Hollybank Road, Drumcondra, had called to the nursing-home on the night of 14 June. She was purported to have had tea with Molly O'Grady at the time when O'Grady was supposed to be in Meath. Why did O'Shaughnessy not turn up to give such evidence? It would have been crucial in getting Molly off the hook. O'Shaughnessy was indeed a reputable witness and one can only surmise that the notoriety of the case and indeed of the defendants at this stage prevented her from attending. After all she was a woman in a job that dealt with the public and she could not face the publicity and hope to remain in employment.

The jury retired and after one hour returned the verdict. John F. Buchanan, the foreman of the jury, read its decision. The jury had found the defendants guilty on both charges, the first being the conspiracy charge: that they, Mary Anne Cadden and Mary O'Grady, on or about 14 June 1938 in the County of Meath conspired together to abandon a child under two years, whereby the life of such child would be endangered, or its health permanently injured. The second charge was the one concerning the actual abandonment: that they, Mary Anne Cadden and Mary O'Grady, on 14 June 1938 in the County of Meath unlawfully abandoned a child under the age of two years, whereby its life was endangered, or its health permanently injured, or was likely to be permanently injured.

The attitude of the jury to Molly O'Grady was remarkable. Though it had little or no grounds for dismissing the charges against her, save her own and Mamie's words, they took a highly unusual step. The jury added a rider to their verdict in relation to Molly. It read: 'The jury is unanimously of the opinion that the accused O'Grady was unduly influenced by Cadden and recommend her to the clemency of the Court.'

There was now the question of the other two cases that were pending (Clarke and Hudson) and the state counsel Kevin Haugh asked for leave to consult the attorney-general on the matter. The court reconvened on 12 May and the sentence was delivered. Mamie Cadden was sentenced to one year's imprisonment with hard labour on both counts, the sentences to run concurrently. Molly O'Grady was sentenced to six month's imprisonment on both counts to run consecutively and not to be enforced on her entering a bond for £25 and undertaking to keep the peace for two years. Mr Justice Black was more than sympathetic to her saying: 'The evidence shows you were under the domination – almost hypnotism – of a strong character.'[29] So Molly O'Grady walked free from the court on that day while Mamie Cadden re-entered the black maria which was to take her back alone to Mountjoy Jail for her year's prison sentence.

In a letter written over a decade later, Mamie alleged that the person in the car with her was Kathleen McLoughlin, the self-styled 'social worker' who farmed out babies from Mamie's establishments. With hindsight this seems altogether more likely.

The women's prison was a grim place and since her sentence was one of 'hard labour' rather than the easier 'penal servitude' it was the lowest point in her life. Still a beautiful woman, she was described as having fair hair, hazel eyes and a fair complexion and being five foot three-and-a-half inches tall. Of course she lied about her age putting herself down as thirty-four years when she was in fact forty-seven, but that was Mamie, she never let reality overcome her vanity. She even asked to be allowed wear her own clothes rather than the harsh prison uniform but her request seems to have been denied.[30] She signed herself in as Roman Catholic which was the family religion but even then she could hardly be described as devout, though she did have a visit from Father McCarthy while on remand in 1938.

Now that she had the time it was inevitable that her thoughts would turn to the events of the past year. She began to focus on Charles Boyle and her legal team, who seemed to be the only people to gain financially out of the whole affair. It was Charles Boyle who had taken her through the sale of her house to ensure that adequate moneys were available for his team's fees. She now focused much of her resentment on him and decided to pursue matters on her release. Charles Boyle was certainly well-connected but not necessarily a good defence lawyer. It was true that her legal team didn't put up much of a defence hoping that the circumstantial nature of the evidence against her would not be sufficient for a conviction. But they were wrong. Not for the last time was circumstantial evidence to be enough to convict Mamie Cadden.

The Central Board of Midwives acted quickly to remove Mamie from the profession. On 17 May 1939 the board's secretary, Olive G. Myler, wrote to the Dublin county registrar, Seamus O'Connor, seeking confirmation of the verdict. The board, it stated, would be obliged to take action to remove Mamie from the roll of midwives. This was exactly what it did when it next met on 6 July: Mary Anne Cadden was removed from its 'roll of midwives in Ireland and prohibited from attending women in childbirth'. The notice was delivered on the same day to Mamie in her Mountjoy prison cell by the board's solicitor, Arthur Cox.

This was the final blow for Mamie; education had liberated her from her background of rural austerity. The loss of her money and house could be restored later on but rejection by her profession could not. She was never to re-apply for readmission to her profession though she continued to style herself as 'Nurse Cadden'.

It was symptomatic of the Ireland of the day that the other business of the board that day, 6 July 1939, was to strike off another midwife for performing an abortion. But whatever the board did, it could never do enough to satisfy the authorities who could not abide an independent body ruling an independent profession of women. Within ten years it would be on the verge of being subsumed into An Bord Altranais.

6

A Fresh Start in the 1940s

When Mamie emerged from Mountjoy Jail in early 1940, she headed straight for Dublin Castle where she made a statement of complaint to the gardaí against Charles W. Boyle, now described as her 'former solicitor' (her new solicitors were Murtagh, Fay and Co). It seems she was having difficulty getting back her registers and record books from 183 Lower Rathmines Road as well as all the other exhibits from the trial, which had been lodged by the gardaí with her solicitor.

She temporarily removed herself to Dun Laoghaire where she stayed at the house of her friend, G. Bayley Spencer, at 10 Crosthwaite Park South in rather salubrious circumstances. From here she was to wage war on her former solicitor who in her opinion had sat back, if not colluded with, the prosecution, while she lost everything. She signed a statement that she had received some of the trial exhibits but there remained the question of the nursing-home register. This was hot property, containing as it did the names not only of the clients but also of the medical practitioners who assisted the clients in the nursing-home. It was accepted at the trial that these were some of the leading doctors in Dublin at the time. Somebody as well connected as Charles Boyle might have been very wary of the contents of this book lest it incriminate some of his important friends. Mamie quite genuinely needed the register if she was to salvage some kind of medical job for herself from the wreckage of her career.

The authorities were now following her every move as they were to do for the rest of her life. In September 1940 her new solicitors sought her original statement of complaint to the gardaí concerning Charles Boyle. The commissioner of the garda síochána wrote to the chief state solicitor for advice, who in turn wrote to the attorney-general for his directions on the matter. Maybe her solicitors feared that Mamie had said something compromising in her statement which might be used by Boyle later on in court. Given Mamie's explosive personality, this seems more than likely. The attorney-general wrote back directing that the request for the statement be granted. He even added rather pointedly: 'She seems to have been very harshly treated by her advisors.'[31] The affair was even more complicated in that the attorney-general was Kevin Haugh who had been the state prosecutor in the 1939 trial and would have known Mamie's case well.

The affair dragged into 1941 and Mamie made a complaint in front of Mr Justice Hannan regarding her register. But not for the first time in her career was she her own worst enemy. The attorney-general's office was quite prepared to provide the evidence that the register was handed over to Boyle which presumably, would have forced him to hand it back to Mamie even before a court case. However, instead of letting things develop as they were, Mamie, intent on annoying Boyle to the maximum and letting her wild sense of humour get the better of her commonsense, put an advertisement in the 'Miscellaneous' columns of the *Evening Mail* on

21 January 1941. 'Nurse Cadden', it informed the readers, would soon be 'leaving for London to publish a book on how her solicitor was kidnapped by Charles the Kidnapper.' It could only have referred to Charles Boyle. It was too much for the sedate attorney-general who now styled himself as Kevin O'Hanrahan Haugh: 'I came to the conclusion that this lady has possibly become mental', he wrote. Accordingly he sent a message to Mr Justice Hannan that state intervention was undesirable especially as Charles Boyle might take an action against Miss Cadden, the *Evening Mail*, or both. Thus ended Mamie's chances of getting her register returned.

But she had other things besides Charles Boyle to think about: she had to get herself back in business and start earning a living. She had no money and insufficient credit to purchase new premises and was barred from midwifery anyway. However, there were other related paramedical areas in which she could operate: there was a market for cures for dandruff, skin diseases and especially constipation (about which Ireland seemed fixated. The newspapers advertised cures for the complaint each day, some of which recommended a daily dose of laxative. One can only imagine the havoc a daily dose over a long period caused). Nurse Cadden began to provide enemas and became a very popular practitioner.

However her main service soon switched to abortion provision. In a country and capital city where contraception was forbidden and unavailable the amount of unwanted pregnancies was considerable. It is more than ironic to consider that the state governed in material austerity by Éamon de

Valera, the Taoiseach and in spiritual orthodoxy by John Charles McQuaid, the Catholic archbishop of Dublin, would have a thriving abortion industry. But that's how it was, precipitated by the absolute prohibition and unavailability of contraceptives.

The situation was of course exacerbated by the fact that the world was now in the throes of war. Though Ireland was a neutral nation in the Second World War it suffered many of the privations of the belligerents including widespread shortages and rationing. Furthermore there were travel restrictions between Ireland and Britain which cut down on the number of people who moved between the two countries. Travel was not easy anyway: the boat-train from Dublin to London took about twelve hours and even in first class was quite a gruelling ordeal; in second or third class it was often an uncomfortable and stomach-wrenching experience. Air travel, even when it was available, was only for the wealthy elite. To make matters worse, London was suffering under the Blitz and nightly bombing raids were hardly conducive to encouraging visitors to the city.

Under these conditions the Dublin abortion industry mushroomed. It had always been a thriving part of the medical scene in Dublin and had been part of the nursing-home services provided by Mamie Cadden in Rathmines and by others in many of the other Dublin nursing-homes. However, in her two previous homes the abortion services were additional to the other work, which was mainly related to the care of pregnant women and their newborn children.

Mamie now needed to establish herself in a central area

preferably in or near the city centre for her clientele to access her services. Dublin's medical area was then centred on the beautiful Georgian squares on the southside near government and parliament buildings in Leinster House. At Fitzwilliam Square Dublin's most exclusive and expensive doctors set themselves up in a copy of London's Harley Street. Nearby on Upper Pembroke Street Mamie set up her premises. She rented an extensive basement suite and with most of the medical equipment salvaged from the house in Rathmines she set up shop once more. It was an elegant and busy street and on warm days Mamie would sit outside her door on a wicker chair chatting and joking with the passers-by.

She advertised in the leading evening paper of the time, the *Evening Mail*, which in those pre-television days had an even higher circulation than the morning papers. Its content also seemed to be less high brow with more photos and colour features; just the type of paper one would expect a younger person to read. Her advertisements, which were placed in the medical column of the paper, were elegant and understated and would require decoding to find out their true meaning. One advertisement read as follows: Nurse Cadden, 21 Upper Pembroke Street, Dublin. Male, Female cases treated, hand massages, enemas etc.' In 1944 when questioned by the gardaí she boldly declared, 'I treat VD patients, the pox, that's my job'.

That she did perform 'hand massages, enemas etc' there is no doubt. Her treatment of venereal disease would have been limited in an era before the widespread use of penicillin but it would have given her a good market as the stigma attached to these ills would have driven many sufferers to seek her services rather than risk exposure by attending their family doctor. Notwithstanding all these treatments, there was little doubt what her main business was: the performing of abortions. Just round the corner was her main rival, William Coleman, who had his abortion clinic on Merrion Square, while the busiest one in Dublin at the time was on Parkgate Street. One can be sure that the eminent consultants of Fitzwilliam Square, with their close connections with the top echelons of Church and State were not too impressed, not that their opinion would have mattered a jot to Mamie.

In England at the time abortion was illegal or at least very restricted. The law would not be liberalised until 1967 and it is from England that we get the term 'backstreet abortionist' which is often used to describe Mamie Cadden. It conjures up ideas of backlanes, furtiveness and squalor. However, this was not how Mamie operated at all. She always chose a prominent street location for her business, as up-market and fashionable as possible. Furthermore, everyone seemed to know what her business was and she enjoyed a great social life mixing with the cream of Dublin society.

Just a year out of Mountjoy Jail and Mamie was in business again with a growing client list. In the face of adversity she had rebuilt her life and started again. She had kept her car, the red MG sportscar which was garaged for the duration of the war as petrol was virtually unavailable but which she would get on the road again at war's end. Things were not nearly as good as they were when she had the nursing-home in Rathmines but they were getting there. Who could tell what opportunities would next be open to her? She had taken them all on and survived. She had shown them that Mamie Cadden could not be put down that easily.

7

Ellen's Story

Ellen Thompson was a twenty-year-old domestic servant from Ballinteer at the foot of the Dublin Mountains.[32] She worked for Mr and Mrs Larry Doyle at 26 Frankfort Park in nearby Dundrum, an outer suburb of Dublin and had done since 1938 when she left school. It was not an unusual situation. Ireland in the 1940s had a profusion of domestic servants. Even the lower-middle-class houses of teachers and bank clerks had a live-in servant called 'the maid' who answered the door and did the drudge work in an era before labour-saving domestic appliances like the washing machine and the vacuum cleaner became commonplace. Most of all she gave a certain status to the household. To have a maid was a sign of prosperity and of that most valued of commodities in 1940s Ireland: respectability.

Domestic servants were paid a pittance and worked long hours sometimes with just a half day off a week. But there was little or no choice in the labour market for young unskilled women. It was either domestic service or the boat-train to England where there was plenty of assembly-line factory work. But in wartime with the bombings and the shortages, this probably did not seem like a very enviable alternative. Ellen Thompson was lucky in that she worked quite near her mother's house in Ballinteer Cottages, a county council development of 112 comfortable houses, so she had plenty of support, always somewhere to go on her half-days and no need to be lonely at all.

But in October 1944 Ellen was 'in trouble', she was pregnant; a single girl's greatest nightmare. Pregnancy could result in loss of employment and loss of 'respectability', which might take away a girl's marriage prospects forever. In some cases the family might disown such a girl. For a working-class girl like Ellen it might mean incarceration in one of the dreaded Magdalen Homes which was tantamount to slavery and penitence, sometimes for life, accompanied by the loss of the baby to the institution. Ellen Thompson was adamant. She was not going to go down this road of subjection and misery.

On Sunday afternoon, 22 October, she boarded the bus from near her employer's house in Dundrum having first had her dinner. She had been working all morning and this was her half-day. She travelled to Ranelagh where she took the No 11 bus into the city alighting at Upper Pembroke Street where Nurse Cadden had her flat cum medical rooms. Ellen crossed the street and went up the steps of No. 21. She pressed the second last bell from the bottom. It had 'Nurse' written beside it. Ellen was later to claim that she arrived at Nurse Cadden's front door on foot of an advertisement she had read in the *Evening Mail*. She said she had been on her knees in front of the fireplace at 26 Frankfort Avenue in Dundrum screwing up bits of paper to light the fire when her eyes fell on an *Evening Mail* advertisement in its medical column which read: 'All surgical, medical ailments treated

by Nurse Cadden, 21 Upper Pembroke Street.' The paper,
she said, was about two years old at the time.

She had been 'keeping company' with boys as she rather
quaintly described it and had sex with some of them. She had
missed her period in August and September and now feared
that she might be pregnant. And so she began that lonely,
desperate but brave bus journey, all alone, a twenty-year-old
in search of a way out of a dreadful dilemma. Nurse Cadden's
apartment was in the basement of the large Georgian house
and had a small yard to the front, just below street level. The
steps overlooked the yard. When Ellen rang the bell a woman came into this area and looked up. Soon afterwards the
front door was opened by a lady with blonde curls over which
she wore a rust-coloured hat with a feather across it and a
white doctor's coat. When Ellen asked for Nurse Cadden the
lady at the door told her that she was Nurse Cadden and
asked her into the hall. Inside, Nurse Cadden asked Ellen her
business and when Ellen answered that she wanted to talk to
her in private she said that she would have to wait a while as
she already had patients and would deal with her when they
left. Sunday was obviously a busy day for Mamie Cadden.
Shortly afterwards two ladies came upstairs accompanied by
Nurse Cadden and as she let them out the front door she
reminded them to remember her number the next time.

She asked Ellen to follow her and they went down the
stairs to the basement flat. The stairway was dark and Mamie
carried a torch to light the way. They went into the main
room at the front of the house which was all set up as a con-
sulting/operating room. The window blind was down and the

room was lit by an electric light. It was about ten minutes past four in the afternoon. Mamie asked Ellen to state her business and Ellen told her that she had not had her periods since the second last week in July. Nurse Cadden said she would examine her and on Mamie's directions Ellen removed her clothes, first her coat, then her mauve scarf which had been a present from her mother. She stripped down to her vest and lay on her back on the bed with her feet raised on a chair. Mamie examined her new patient using a duck-billed speculum and a probe that she kept in a large jug near the bed. She had seemed so composed and brave so far but then said that she hoped she wouldn't be getting any needles as she had a dread of them since she was inoculated when she was a child. Mamie reassured her saying that she did not use needles and that only her rival, Mr Coleman, of Merrion Square used them. Ellen felt no pain but said that she felt something rattling inside her. When the examination was complete Mamie told her that she was three months pregnant, which hardly came as a surprise.

Mamie told her patient that she would clean out her front and back passages and began to prepare the douche with a mixture of water and the disinfectant Dettol, and used warm water from the adjoining scullery for the enema. She already had a stand in place over the bed from which to drop the solution and had a rubber sheet on the bed and a basin on the floor. Several instruments and labelled bottles were on shelves and on tables around the room. There was a commode behind a screen at the head of the bed that Ellen used after her enema. When these procedures were complete she was asked to resume her previous position on the bed. Mamie again inserted the duck-billed speculum and assured Ellen that she would 'get the bugger the hell out of that'. She inserted something else. It was called a 'sea-tangle tent' and its aim was to induce abortion. Ellen claimed she did not know what this was, though she would of course have guessed its purpose.

Sea-tangle tents were sold in bottles of six around the corner in the medical suppliers at 95 Merrion Square. They were slender rods usually with fine string attached. The strings were for the purpose of their removal. They were inserted into the passage between the vagina and the body of the womb. This passage is normally closed. After its insertion the sea-tangle tent would absorb moisture and would expand. This expansion would further open the passage. In the case of an operation this would allow for the insertion of an instrument. In the case of a pregnant woman however, the insertion of a sea-tangle tent, if left in position, would frequently cause abortion.[33] This was Mamie Cadden's method of dealing with Ellen Thompson's crisis pregnancy. Mamie told her patient that the item she had inserted would come away in a few days and that she must keep it and anything else that came away and to return with it all. She must let no one see these items. Ellen hardly needed any prompting.

When the operation was over the two women stood talking for a few minutes. Ellen contended that she then informed Nurse Cadden that she was a domestic servant and could not pay her much. According to Ellen, Nurse Cadden accepted this and said that when Ellen returned they could work something out. This is where Ellen's story begins to fall down. Even Nurse Cadden's greatest supporters would never claim that she did her work for anything other than cash paid beforehand or on the spot. In fact Ellen was later to recall that there was a sign on the wall saying 'No credit given'. The idea that the hard-headed Nurse Cadden would not have demanded her fee beforehand is unlikely. It is also unlikely that a girl like Ellen would know only too well the 'cash for treatment' nature of Irish medicine at the time. It is highly unlikely that she would have entered any medical establishment in 1940s Ireland, other than a state dispensary, without the cash to pay for her treatment.

This incident must throw doubt on other aspects of her story that initially sounded plausible. Could she really have found out about the clinic just by reading a two-year-old paper with a very ambiguous advertisement? After all she was a twenty-year-old girl with little worldly experience. How did she come to interpret 'Male and female cases treated' as code for 'abortions performed'? If she did not come by this information on her own then what experienced person led her to it? Her story about having intercourse with several 'boys' in the locality somehow does not ring true either. A well-brought-up young girl from a stable background with a job that allowed her such little time off would hardly be in a situation where she would have even had time for this. It would be twelve years before there were possible answers to these and to other questions that Ellen's story would throw up.

When Ellen got dressed again she fixed her hair in front

of the mirror in the same room. The blind on the window was let up and the light was switched off. Nurse Cadden's work for the day was finished. She led her patient back up the staircase and out the same way she entered. Mamie was still wearing the white coat and the hat with the feather. She had kept her hat on during the operation! She also wore glasses; her eyesight was beginning to deteriorate noticeably. It was now about 5 p.m.; the whole procedure had taken a mere fifty minutes. Ellen walked down to Cuffe Street and got a bus to Dundrum and from there she got another bus to her mother's house in Ballinteer.

8

A Girl in Trouble

Ellen had her tea back in her mother's house in Ballinteer Cottages. Her mother never suspected a thing; Ellen just told her that she was in town looking at the shops. Feeling very tired but quite relieved she walked back to her employers' house in Dundrum at about 11 p.m. – the 'maid' was expected to live in her employer's house. On her way back to Frankfort Park she missed her scarf and realised she had left it in Nurse Cadden's flat. She had taken it off with her coat and left it on the chair near the bed. She must remember to ask for it when she returned next Sunday, she thought. She had burned one end of it in front of the fire when she had tried to dry it out after getting caught in the rain one day. She had cut off the end with the scorch mark so it would be easy to recognise. Her mother would miss it, though she could always say she left it on the bus.

She felt a bit tired on Monday but otherwise all right and was very hopeful that everything would be fine; all she had to do was wait, as Nurse Cadden had instructed. She hoped that nothing would happen before Sunday as that was the only free time she would have off to take the stuff back into Pembroke Street. She didn't sleep well on Monday night and by Tuesday morning she felt poorly and knew something was seriously wrong. She became weak and thought she might faint and fall down. She walked carefully and slowly into the kitchen to get a drink of water but was unable to pour one for herself. After a few minutes she felt a bit better but decided to go upstairs to her bedroom and lie down.

She was soon convulsed with severe stomach pains and called her employer, Mrs Doyle. Mrs Doyle called for the doctor immediately, who arrived at about 10.40 a.m. The doctor spoke to her but did not conduct a physical examination. She told them that if things did not get better she would return in the evening. The doctor had no idea at this stage that Ellen was pregnant. When things did not improve during the day the doctor returned that evening at around 6 p.m. This time she did conduct a physical examination and discovered the strings from the sea-tangle tent in her vagina. She tried to remove it by tugging at the strings that were attached to it for this purpose but it was so firmly lodged that the strings broke away in her hand. All through this time poor Ellen was suffering from dreadful stomach pains. The doctor knew now that she was dealing with an abortion operation that had gone terribly wrong. She summoned an ambulance and Ellen was taken to the National Maternity Hospital in Holles Street. Ellen's mother, Elizabeth, who had now arrived on the scene, accompanied her in the ambulance, as did Mrs Doyle. It was discovered that Ellen was suffering from peritonitis: an inflammation of the abdominal wall that could have led to death if left untreated. She was operated on that night by Dr Alex Spain. She was kept in the hospital for sixteen days and when discharged was back to full health. She was a strong young woman and the long-term consequences of the incident were likely to be more psychological than physical. The consequences for Mamie Cadden though were likely to be catastrophic.

For the hospital authorities there was a procedure to be followed. The hospital in Holles Street was then and still is a hospital that operated under Catholic medical ethics. They were dealing with a person on whom an abortion operation had been attempted. This was a criminal offence under the Offences Against the Person Act of 1861. The very next morning, Wednesday 25 October 1944, they informed the police. The police promptly arrived in the hospital and took a statement from Ellen, still in her bed and weak after the operation to remove the sea-tangle tent. The poor girl must have been terrified that she might have been put on some charge and she cooperated completely with the police in identifying Mamie Cadden as the person who had inserted the sea-tangle tent.

Inspector Martin O'Neill and Sergeant King, who had interviewed Ellen, then headed over to 21 Upper Pembroke Street where Mamie was taken by complete surprise. She was unflustered and denied the charge of performing an abortion on Ellen Thompson. 'I don't know her and I don't know what you're talking about,' she insisted vehemently, going typically on the offensive. 'I treat VD patients, the pox, that's my job.' But the evidence of an abortion clinic was all around her. All her instruments, her medicines and equipment were scattered in profusion around the flat. Mamie was never a tidy woman. She was arrested on the spot, charged by a magistrate and remanded to Mountjoy Jail, from which she had been released only a little over four years previously. Now as she stared at its dreary walls she must have felt a deep despair. It was typical of her spirit however that even now she did not give in. No abortion had taken place, how could they prove that Ellen Thompson had ever visited her on the day in question? She would fight them in court, she would never give in. But her health began to show signs of the enormous strain she was under. For three weeks in a row she could not appear in court to answer the charges due to illness. The prison doctor, W. A. Cooke, certified her as being unfit to attend due to phlebitis – inflammation of a vein. Mamie was beginning to suffer from varicose veins.

This time however the police had a witness and would not have to depend on circumstantial evidence as they had in the Meath case six years earlier. Ellen Thompson was to be their star witness and the poor girl, terrified as she must have been, was hardly likely to be anything other than co-operative. It is not difficult to imagine how intimidated the weak and sick young woman must have been. On 2 November her baby was aborted in Holles Street. On 29 November, just five weeks after her visit to the clinic she identified Mamie at an identity parade in the Bridewell garda station. To make matters worse, she identified her mauve scarf as the one she had left behind in Pembroke Street on that fateful Sunday. Mamie had been foolish or careless enough to take it with her in her suitcase and it was soon discovered by Inspector O'Neill.

Things looked bleak for Mamie Cadden as Christmas approached and she prepared to spend her second festive season behind bars. Worse still, the prospect of a term in prison, even longer than her previous one, must have filled her with horror. In the prison register she is described as single, Roman Catholic and able to read and write. She has fair hair, hazel eyes and a fresh complexion. She again performs some subtraction on her age that originally appears as forty and is crossed out to read fifty-three years: her correct age. The papers all reported her as being forty. That must have pleased her. She weighed 11 stone and 11 pounds, quite a lot for a woman of 5 feet, 3 $^1/_2$ inches. In spite of her privations, on 21 December she made her long awaited statement.

Yes, she remembered Sunday 22 October 1944 well. Her cousin, Patrick Martin, had visited her in the morning. He lived on the northside of Dublin at 29 Beaumont over the Fairview Egg Stores. She asked him to stay for lunch but he said that he was expected home for dinner. They arranged to meet later that day, he returned at about 3.30 p.m. and they went walking around town looking for a film to attend. All the picture houses were full though so they had to content themselves with some window-shopping which must have been a bleak enough activity at the height of the war. Later they went to the Gresham Hotel for dinner, presumably Patrick's second of the day. A waiter there informed them that all the tables were taken and suggested that they return later. They went for a few drinks in the Tower Bar in Talbot Street and after three or four drinks returned to the Gresham Hotel where they had dinner and were the last or the second last to leave.

Her statement tells rather a comfortable story of life in

Dublin during the war when other European capitals were being bombed daily. The Gresham Hotel was one of the state's premier institutions and was the height of fashion and style. Young girls would take afternoon tea there to learn social mixing and deportment and, with the Shelbourne, it was the hotel of choice for celebrities visiting the city. To indicate a habit of dining regularly there on a Sunday evening, as Mamie did, was to make a statement not only about her social life but also about her ability to afford to dine with the top layer in Dublin society. And she had witnesses to prove her story. Patrick Martin would corroborate it all, as would James Smith, a waiter in the Gresham. Charles Hoban, a neighbour from 13 Upper Pembroke Street would testify as to how he had visited Mamie and met no one but her cousin, Patrick.

She added that after the identity parade in the Bridewell garda station in November she did recognise Ellen as the girl who had visited her in August suffering from a white discharge. This was Mamie at her bitchiest. The reference to 'a white discharge' was undoubtedly a suggestion that Ellen Thompson had contracted gonorrhoea, had been promiscuous and had come to her for a remedy. Mamie said that she had refused to treat her or to refer her to a doctor on that occasion, as she was unable to pay the fee in advance. This contrasts significantly with Ellen's alleged account of Mamie's generosity in October when she claimed that Mamie had told her not to bother about money as they could arrange things later.

On 21 December 1944 Mamie Cadden was returned for

trial by District Justice Farrell. It seemed that her trial was to
be part of a campaign to shut down Dublin's thriving abortion service to which wartime travel restrictions had given
an extra boost. The early 1940s was to see the greatest on-
slaught against abortion in Ireland since the foundation of
the state, events hardly unconnected with the start of the
episcopate of John Charles McQuaid which had commenced
in 1940. He was a deeply conservative prelate especially in
matters relating to women's fertility and sexuality. Abortion
was to be expunged from the face of Catholic Ireland. Mamie
had been a major practitioner almost since her release from
Mountjoy Jail four years previously and could expect no
mercy. The years 1942–6 saw the highest number of prosecutions or investigations concerning abortion in the history of
the state. They totalled twenty-five.[34] The stories of Mr
Coleman and Dr Ashe of Merrion Square will illustrate the
situation. This new Ireland was one where Catholic ethics
relating to fertility matters were to be rigorously imposed.
The 'laissez faire' times of the 1920s and 1930s were over.
Now it was to be a Catholic state for a Catholic people. In
such a state there would be no room for abortion services.

9

The Talented Mr Coleman and
the Well-Connected Dr Ashe

Mamie Cadden was far from being the only supplier of abortions in Ireland in the middle of the twentieth century. In spite of the heavy anti-permissive atmosphere there were many pregnancies outside marriage and indeed there were many unwanted pregnancies inside marriage. As well as Mamie's busy clinic on Upper Pembroke Street there was an even more extensive one around the corner in fashionable Merrion Square owned and run by the shady and enterprising William Henry Coleman, who lived at No. 25 with his wife and mother. The houses on Merrion Square are substantial Georgian four-storey-over-basement houses. Besides his family's living quarters and a flat he had let out, Coleman could accommodate clients who wanted residential care after their operation. His clinic was well-known and, as it was near Holles Street, there was a running joke that cheeky bus conductors would ask women alighting at the Merrion Square bus stop, 'Are you for Holles Street or for Mr Coleman?'

He was very different to Mamie Cadden especially in that he had no medical qualification whatever. Even Mamie's greatest critics could never find fault with her professional treatment of her patients.

Coleman was a different operator altogether. He was an

electrician with a criminal record. In 1933 he had been convicted of arson, attempts to procure money under false pretences and a bankruptcy-related charge, and had received
three years penal servitude.[35] In 1936 he established his medical practice in Merrion Square and it thrived. A brilliant
self-publicist, he made great use of advertisements in the
Evening Mail and attracted quite an extensive clientele.

In his newspaper advertisements he offered to deal with
'psychological, nervous, sexual troubles' or 'advice on marriage difficulties'.[36] These advertisements sometimes cost him
up to £70 per annum and must have been quite effective in
drumming up business for him. His records of June 1936 to
1944 show that he treated such conditions as 'venereal disease, masturbation, inferiority complex, nerves, superfluous
hairs, impotence, and constipation'.[37] He kept quite extensive records, something that Mamie Cadden would never
think of. Regardless of their reasons for attending him, these
patients made a very substantial client list for William Henry
Coleman.

That he was not a qualified medical man did not seem to
matter much to his clientele. An untrained doctor was not
looked on with such suspicion in the Ireland of the mid-
twentieth century. William Coleman was obviously a man
with some medical knowledge even if he had no formal or
academic training in the subject. He had an x-ray machine
in his surgery and acted as radiographer, taking and develop-
ing the plates himself. This was very advanced technology
for the Ireland of the time. He x-rayed all his pregnant
patients, something that would be considered unheard of and

dangerous in later years. The x-ray machine must have been almost unique in Irish surgeries at the time. He also had a medical library of some eighteen books that played a part later at his trial.

Despite his large list of psychosexual patients, Coleman had another speciality: abortion. In 1937, he had been found not guilty on an abortion charge and continued to function with impunity. In fact it was in the early 1940s that his advertising and notoriety reached its peak. Travel to Britain during the war years was difficult and Coleman was there to take advantage of the extra numbers requiring abortions in Ireland. It was a 'nod and a wink' situation for William Coleman instead of the blunt outspokenness of Mamie Cadden: when he had conducted his examination of the pregnant woman using his famous x-ray machine, he would inform them that they had a tubal pregnancy which would not come to term and that he could solve the problem before it developed further possibly causing complications and endangering the woman's life. If the woman agreed then she could have the operation performed in three sessions with him for a cost of around £70 or she could stay in one of the apartments in the house for the week after the operation for £120. This situation continued unhindered until 1944. It is hard to believe that the wider medical profession was not aware of what was going on.

Once when a dissatisfied patient threatened to report Coleman to Archbishop McQuaid, Coleman was sufficiently concerned about the threat to keep an exact record of his conversation with the woman. McQuaid had direct control over the city's Catholic hospitals. These were in a good position to look out for and report any cases where they suspected that their patients had abortions. There were many complications possible after abortions and if treated in one of these hospitals then the medical personnel would, if they saw fit, be in a prime position to report any patients who had the operation. This was to be the downfall of Coleman and indeed the same stratagem was to play its part in the downfall of Mamie Cadden too. Archbishop McQuaid himself came from a medical background, his father and sister were both doctors and as such he would have a unique insight into affairs concerning pregnancy and fertility. Indeed it is fair to say that during his long episcopal career his interest in fertility, women's sexuality and childbirth seemed to border on the obsessive.

On 13 April 1944 Coleman was arrested and his extensive files seized. On 2 May 1944 he was charged with using an instrument to procure an abortion on Maureen Patricia Brabazon and on Judy Marjorie Bolton.

Brabazon had paid £75 for her abortion. Judy Bolton, who worked in the Country Shop, a restaurant on Stephen's Green, had borrowed her £70 for the operation from Hugh Shearman, a Trinity College student from County Down. Hugh Shearman was in later life to become a leading figure in the Unionist Party in Northern Ireland, a thorough conservative he wrote a Unionist apologia entitled *Not an Inch*. Judy, though only nineteen, was married to a twenty-three-year-old student at Trinity, Alphonsus Mifsud. Both women had serious complications after the operation and Judy Bolton had been removed to the Meath hospital with a serious haemorrhage.

In the raid on Coleman's surgery in Merrion Square, his files, his medical equipment, including his foot stirrups, his medical books and his supplies of medicines were seized, as possible incriminating exhibits. In his desk was found a piece of writing in which he described, in the first person, abortions performed on two sisters. Coleman claimed this was a short story he was writing but much use was made of it in court. Supplies of Ergot, the abortifacient, were also seized. He had large supplies in tablet as well as in powder form and he also had supplies of Femergin, which was a preparation of Ergot. The authorities however were unable to prove that these supplies were not around from the previous raid on the premises as Ergot was a very stable and long-lasting drug. Coleman, never short of an excuse, claimed that he used it in connection with his photographic work.

Alphonsus Mifsud, supposedly a student from Gibraltar, though the name is more common in Malta, gave evidence with a frankness that would have been impossible for an Irishman of his age. He was not on speaking terms with his parents and was thus without funds. He first had sex with Judy in Galway in 1940 and had been using Gymonmin, a chemical contraceptive that he had purchased from a fellow student from Northern Ireland.[38] Judy, who lived on Merrion Square with her mother, had ceased to practise as a Catholic four-and-a-half years previously. The couple got married in the registry office the day after Coleman was arrested. The prosecution alleged that this was to prevent Judy giving evidence against him; the evidence of wife against husband being inadmissible in court.

William Coleman did not help himself when he was caught by Warder Scannell trying to pass a note to his wife after a visit to Mountjoy Jail on 28 April. When the visit ended they shook hands and as they did two notes fell from his hands. The warder picked them up and refused to return them to Coleman. Instead he handed them over to the police where they were included in the evidence against Coleman. The notes asked that the women to be called as witnesses be reminded that no instruments were used on them and that they did not hand over large sums of money. The notes also asked that an accountant in Killiney, a Mr McCrea, be asked for the bail money as William Coleman was again declared bankrupt on 14 July 1944.

Coleman's defence was that the abortions that took place happened naturally and were not induced by him. The prosecution really went to extremes in describing Coleman and his trade: 'No fouler being has ever crossed the threshold of the dock; your Lordship has never had before you a man so consummate in his infamy, so depraved and vile in his occupation and in so many aspects of his life,' said J. A. McCarthy (Mamie's former counsel). The judge, Mr Davitt, was clearly exasperated by the whole proceedings and referring to this and the other related cases in 1944 he moaned: 'It is a melancholy reflection that for the past few weeks I have been trying these cases and nothing else.'

After a trial that lasted from 10 to 20 July 1944 he was found guilty and sentenced to fifteen years penal servitude, a rather harsh sentence by any standard. Judge Davitt was quite explicit in his view of abortion and the severity of the sentence he would impose: 'The offence of criminal abortion is akin to murder and justice in this case demands an exemplary sentence.'

But the resourceful Coleman was not finished yet and he appealed the verdict and the sentence. In November 1944 at the Court of Criminal Appeal the verdict and sentence were quashed and a retrial was ordered with the state to pay the costs.[39] The defendant, however, was to remain in custody. One of the grounds for this was that the judge had read a passage to the jury from one of the books seized in Mr Coleman's office. The book was *Parry on Criminal Abortion* and the passage claimed that perpetrators might offend again.

The re-trial took place in February 1945 before Chief Justice Overend, president of the High Court. The chief state solicitor asked that the sentence be increased. Coleman was again found guilty but had his sentence reduced to seven years penal servitude. He appealed again in June 1945 but failed. In 1952, when he had completed his sentence, the family moved on from Merrion Square and Coleman disappeared from public view.

*

1944 saw the breaking up of another extensive abortion service based, like William Coleman's, on Dublin's fashionable Merrion Square though the operations themselves took place mainly in Parkgate Street.[40] The most prominent person charged was a senior and elderly doctor, James Ashe, who practised from No. 19 and described himself with upper-

class modesty as a 'physician'. He was also a medical examiner at the matrimonial division of the High Court. Dr
Ashe was at the centre of what would now be referred to as
an abortion referral service but what was then referred to by
its opponents as 'an abortion ring'. In autumn 1943 the
breaking up of the network began when Christopher
Williams and Mary Moloney were charged with procuring
abortions. They operated their clinic out of a house in
Parkgate Street near the main train station for the west of
the country, Kingsbridge. It was a substantial operation and
Moloney was charged on nine counts of abortion. They
jointly performed the operations but had other accomplices.
Mr Williams, a chemist, and the widowed Mrs Moloney who
was his companion, pleaded guilty. They had been living
together since 1938.

At the end of their trial Judge Cahir Davitt delivered a
stern rebuke. He said there were no mitigating circumstances
in Moloney's defence, that she had no qualifications whatever, and if things had gone wrong she might have been facing a murder charge. Inspector Martin O'Neill said that Mary
Moloney was bold and defiant in the face of the charge and
had even asked her twelve-year-old daughter to assist in the
operations. Williams, the judge thought, had been just as
guilty as Moloney. He noted regretfully that her clients were
girls 'from the better class from the country and the city'.
The prosecution was led by Richard McLoughlin.

Moloney's sentence was harsh in the extreme and acknowledged as such by the judge. She was sentenced to ten
years in jail. It is doubtful if Moloney, aged forty-seven,

would have survived such a sentence with penal servitude. At least she could be forgiven for fearing the harshness of the years ahead. Christopher Williams got seven years. These harsh sentences may have been the reasons for what happened next: Mary Moloney and Christopher Williams started to inform on their contacts and their agents. Perhaps they hoped for more lenient treatment in Mountjoy, perhaps they hoped for a reduction in their harsh sentences or an early parole. When asked in court of their motivation all Williams could say was that the gardaí said they wanted 'more cases' and he thought it right to help them out! Whatever inducements given or offered certainly worked. Almost immediately they began to give evidence against their accomplices, with spectacular results for the gardaí and disastrous results for the abortion services and the people involved in Dublin.

Several agents had sent clients to them including the famous Dr Ashe. The abortions cost between £100 and £120 – an absolute fortune in the 1940s when a working man's wage was £5 a week. The agents took £10 to £20 each along the way for their referral services. Among those arrested was Dr Ashe who appeared before Dublin Circuit Criminal Court between 24 and 26 July with Edward Cecil Flynn (proprietor of a shop called Paris Gowns and a friend of Ashe's from childhood) on five charges: four of abortion and one of conspiracy to commit abortion. The abortion charges related to Mary Davison, Teresa Andreucetti, Louise Moro and Karmel Murtagh. The conspiracy charge linked them with Christopher Williams and Mary Moloney in the abortion referral service. Moloney and Williams appeared as state witnesses.

The first charge that was dealt with related to Teresa Andreucetti; the jury found Edward Flynn guilty of 'intent to procure the miscarriage and the unlawful use of an instrument or some other means at an unknown date in 1941'. The jury however refused to convict Dr Ashe and he was allowed out on continuing bail. The verdict seems to have broken Edward Flynn and he pleaded guilty to counts two and four relating to Louise Moro and Karmel Murtagh. He was sentenced to eight years penal servitude from 31 July 1944. Flynn came out worse than any of the defendants in these years and he seems to be the one who fought least against the charges against him.

The spotlight now shifted to Dr Ashe. He was the big fish. This was no backstreet abortionist: Dr Ashe was a Merrion Square physician who could expect the cream of Irish society in his clientele. He also represented the liberal Protestant and Unionist elite whose place in Irish society was tenuous after independence. His next-door neighbour was Sir James Craig, TD for Trinity College and its professor of medicine.

In 1917, Dr Ashe's namesake, Thomas Ashe, had died after being force-fed while on hunger strike with other Republican prisoners in Mountjoy Jail. His funeral was attended by some 30,000 people. Dr Ashe was not impressed and wrote to the papers to inform the readership that he was not related to 'the late Mr Thomas Ashe'.[41] Now twenty-seven years later a little revenge was played out as Thomas Ashe's sister, who had been deeply insulted by Dr Ashe's 1917 letter, wrote to the papers. She would like to inform readers, she wrote, that she was in no way related to the Dr James Ashe at present appearing before the courts.

The trials of those arrested on foot of Moloney and Williams' evidence now reached their climax from 20–24 November 1944 when the trial of Dr James Ashe continued. Of the five charges originally presented against him and Edward Cecil Flynn only one was proceeded with on this occasion. It was the charge of intent to procure an abortion on Louise Moro in September 1941. Now the state could call not only Moloney and Williams, who had appeared against Edward Flynn, but Flynn himself who, now serving his sentence, was called to give evidence against his former friend and associate.

The elderly Dr Ashe was no pushover however and if the authorities expected an easy conviction they were to be sorely disappointed. Already found not guilty on the charge relating to Mrs Andreucetti he put up a spirited defence. Kingsmill Moore, later to be a distinguished judge himself, led the defence team which included James D'Arcy. Dr Ashe pleaded not guilty. The presiding judge was Mr Wyse-Power, a member of a well-known Protestant Republican family; the judge's religion may have been a help to Dr Ashe when it came to handing down the sentence.

The witnesses for the defence constituted a *Who's Who* of the Dublin medical and Protestant elite. They were: Dr Alex Spain, who was master of Holles Street from 1942 to 1948; Henry Dockrell, the Fine Gael TD for Dublin South since 1932 and son of the former Unionist MP, Sir Maurice Dockrell; Dr Frederick Gill, FRCSI, of Fitzwilliam Place; Rev William Anderson of Pembroke Park; Major John Joseph

Tynan; Sir Robert William Tate; and Mary Josephine Cruise.
Though the jury could not fail to be impressed by the over-
whelmingly Protestant and establishment nature of the witnesses, they could have provoked a hostile reaction from a
Catholic jury in a society where business life was still dominated by a Protestant elite. Superintendent George Lawlor
gave evidence for the prosecution and Detective-Sergeant
Michael Wymes was in charge of the investigation.

The story of the Dr Ashe conviction starts with a female
patient who visited him in 1941 with her husband. The woman was pregnant and already had seven children. The
husband pleaded with Dr Ashe not to allow his wife to come
to full term with the pregnancy as she had almost died as a
result of her last birth. Furthermore, he was much older than
she and not in good health and should he die, he didn't wish
his wife to be left with a newborn baby. Dr Ashe wrote
Edward Cecil Flynn's name on a piece of paper and handed
it to her. She went to Flynn and eventually ended up with
Mrs Moloney who performed an abortion. Her husband died
soon afterwards and three days after he was buried the
detectives arrived at her door, on foot of information from
Moloney and Williams investigating her abortion. In the
witness box she was harassed by the prosecuting counsel until, like a participant in a Moscow show trial the unfortunate
woman was forced to declare that she had done wrong.

The trial of the elderly Dr Ashe lasted a full week. Like
William Coleman the defendant was not going to go without
a fight. Nevertheless on 24 November the jury found him
guilty but recommended leniency on account of his age. His

sentence was handed down on 4 December 1944: he was given eighteen calendar months from 24 November 1944 with special hospital treatments. In January 1945 George Murnahan for the attorney-general informed the court that he would not further prosecute on counts four and five: the abortion charges relating to Karmel Murtagh and the conspiracy charge.

*

The jailing of William Henry Coleman, Dr Ashe, Mrs Moloney and Christopher Williams were major victories for the campaign to close down the Dublin abortion clinics. Charges were also brought against other accomplices or agents like Annie Robinson of Upper Rathmines Road, George McCabe of St Helen's Road in Booterstown, and Charles Brocklebank, a shopkeeper of Fownes Street. Brocklebank tried to commit suicide while awaiting trial.[42] Also involved was an acting member of the gardaí who was charged with attempting to procure an abortion for his girlfriend.[43] Mrs Moloney was alleged to have travelled over to Rathmines to Annie Robinson's flat to do the operation. The charge against him was dismissed.

Thus were the major practitioners on the Dublin abortion circuit dealt with. It was harsh justice. Polite society was shocked and couldn't wait to distance itself from these events. *The Irish Times*, in an editorial on 2 August 1944, entitled 'Moral Standards' explained how it only published the stories of these operations for the good of society. It put in its disclaimer: 'Publication of such reports gives us no pleasure. On the contrary we share to the full the horror and disgust that are felt by all decent people at such sordid disclosures.' Still, *The Irish Times* was the only paper at the time to give any detailed coverage to what really was going on in the country with regard to abortion and the closure of the clinics. Between 1942 and 1946 there were a total of twenty-five recorded cases of investigations and prosecutions. Only one important player now remained: Mary Anne Cadden.

10

Mamie's Turn

Mamie Cadden was in a different category to William Henry Coleman or to the Parkgate Street abortionists. She was a trained midwife and everyone recognised her as such. She held on to her title even after she had been removed from the register of midwives in 1939.[44] Furthermore, arising from her professional qualification and reputation many, if not most, of her referrals came from doctors. They trusted her expertise and qualifications. The other abortionists of the 1940s had a wide and secret network for referrals which was dominated by people with whom the women had commercial transactions. Thus we find that Edward Cecil Flynn and Charles Brocklebank were shopkeepers selling ladies apparel, businesses that brought them into contact with women on a continuing basis.

She was startlingly different too from Dr James Ashe. Whereas he was on the top of the social scale with Dublin's upper echelons in his client list, Mary Anne Cadden was truly the abortionist to the new independent Ireland – to de Valera's Ireland. Since her time running the nursing-home in Rathmines her patients had included the wives of farmers, gardaí and shopkeepers – in fact the emerging Irish middle- and lower-middle-class. Though in her fifty-third year she admitted only to being forty and was still making her mark socially in Dublin. Mamie was not a blushing flower as the denizens of the Gresham or Shelbourne Hotels could testify.

The forthcoming trial on the charge of procuring an abortion for Ellen Thompson was to be about much more than Mamie Cadden. There were people to be protected: the general public had to be kept from the knowledge of the extent of abortion in Catholic Ireland. Ellen's employer, Larry Doyle, and his wife were upstanding Catholic middle-class citizens and would not be dragged into this, or so the standards of the day dictated. If a single girl working in such a respectable household could get pregnant then all single girls must by implication, be at risk. So the trial was held in camera (that is, not in open court), keeping out the press reporters and thus ensuring the least possible publicity.[45] Ireland was again to be protected from the knowledge of its own dark side.

It didn't really matter to Mamie if the case was held in camera or not. She was the only one who would pay the price, not the father of the child, not the person who sent Ellen to her and certainly not the people who prohibited not only the sale but the knowledge of contraceptives in Ireland. The only good thing about the indictment for Mamie was that she was granted bail of £200 plus two independent sureties of £350 each. At least she could get her affairs in order before the case itself took place in the New Year. The first few months of 1945 were the closing months of the Second World War. The continent's teeming millions were about to be liberated from Nazi tyranny. For Mamie, however, freedom in Europe would coincide with her own incarceration. The months waiting for trial were the worst few months in her life to date. Though at liberty she must have known only too well what was facing her. Or did she? Would she not have taken the boat to England and travelled on to America where she could have claimed citizenship if she realised what was ahead of her? She knew what had happened to the other abortionists who had been operating in Dublin: Mary Moloney, Christopher Williams, Dr Ashe, Cecil Flynn, Charles Brocklebank, Annie Robinson, George McCabe and William Coleman had all been sentenced to jail terms. They were now lodged in Mountjoy Jail and all indications were that she would be following. Yet the mystery and enigma of Mamie which made her stand out from so many of her peers both male and female was she never gave up even against the most overwhelming of odds.

Coleman, McCabe, Dr Ashe and the others were to disappear into the realms of obscurity when they had served their sentences, but not Mamie. She would stand and fight. She would fight to win. Ellen Thompson had come to her, she didn't even advertise anymore for clients. Why should she be punished for peritonitis? It wasn't caused by lack of care or lack of hygiene while the girl was with her. Mamie was scrupulously clean and meticulous about sterilising her instruments. She was a professional, not like the others. Coleman was an electrician! He had a bloody cheek setting himself up in practice, she thought, and advertising in the *Evening Mail* about his treatment of 'marriage difficulties and sexual problems'. Not one doctor or expert had ever testified against Mamie's standards of treatment or hygiene at any time in her life. And yet they were out to get her; they just wanted to end abortion in Dublin, that was it. And what would the young girls in trouble do then? Have their babies and hand them over to the Magdalen Homes? Not bloody likely. Some of those women were driven mad with distress and worry, so much so that they would do away with their babies. What would the authorities think about that? Mamie was always indignant that she should ever be brought to trial.

Her trial did not take place until the week of 23–27 April 1945. She appeared before Judge W. G. Shannon of Clare-mont House, Claremont Road in Sandymount. The trial took place in the Circuit Criminal Court in Chancery Place. The charge was: 'Mary Anna Cadden on the 22nd day of October 1944 in the City of Dublin with intent to procure the miscarriage of a woman named Ellen Thompson unlaw-fully used an instrument or some other unknown means.' The jury, as was the case in the 1939 trial, was all male. The Second World War was in its final few weeks but even given the awesomeness of the international news the newspaper coverage of the trial is surprisingly sparse, especially consid-ering the fact that war news was censored as the government maintained neutrality in press reporting right up to and even after the German surrender. In this atmosphere local news was at a premium, but obviously not for the coverage of abor-tion cases. As this trial was held in camera the newspapers maintained a sort of self-censorship regarding it, reporting only on the verdict and sentence in the final days. Only the racier *Evening Mail* made any attempt at coverage. Compared to the daily coverage of the 1939 trial for the much lesser

charge of child abandonment one cannot help thinking that
there was a deliberate attempt to cover up what, by any cri-
terion, was a newsworthy story. Ireland just could not accept
that it had a thriving abortion service in its capital city and
the general public must be protected from this awful news.

Mamie vehemently denied the charge, denied all knowledge of Ellen Thompson except for a fleeting visit from her
in August 1944. If Mamie was vehement in her story so Ellen
was steadfast in her evidence. The woman who operated on
her was Mamie Cadden. She identified her furniture, her
medical equipment and even her feathered hat and tan
shoes. She was the ideal witness for the prosecution. In vain
did Mamie's defence lawyer, Liam Trant McCarthy, object to
the identity parade as being unfair to his client and to her
treatment at the hands of Inspector O'Neill. The evidence of
her cousin, Patrick Martin, and her good neighbour, Charles
Hoban, could not compete with the innocent but deadly ac-
curate and forensically descriptive evidence of Ellen Thompson.

Dr John McGrath, the state pathologist, gave the forensic
evidence. He had visited the flat at Upper Pembroke Street
on 26 October 1944, the day after Mamie was arrested. He
produced no less than forty-five exhibits including an array
of instruments and medicines that could be used in abortions
including:[46]

> a jar containing a catheter (a narrow tube used for
>   draining)
> a jar of the disinfectant, Dettol,

two large douche tops,
a forceps,
six pairs of scissors,
a broken thermometer,
a scalpel,
five clip forceps,
three dissecting forceps,
two pessaries,
a rubber douche,
a plugging forceps,
a jar containing a speculum and other articles,
a syringe case,
a syringe case containing a tube that had in it three
smaller tubes of atropine sulphate, hyoscyamine sulphate
    and morphine sulphate,
a syringe plunger,
a Higginson syringe,
a douche apparatus with a can of tubing,
a metal catheter and mucus extractor,
a flushing curette which is a spoon-shaped instrument
    for removing tissue from bodily cavities,
a long clamp forceps,
a folding examination table,
a vaginal speculum,
Sulphur thianol tablets,
two hypodermic needles,
two drums containing items for sterilisation
a box containing ampoules,
two white coats,

a jar of the lubricant, Vaseline,

three medical books.

Many of the items were also identified by Ellen Thompson, who seemed to have a photographic memory. Even without the state pathologist's evidence it wouldn't have required the most medically inclined mind to deduce that here was the apparatus of an abortion clinic. Neither he nor any of the other witnesses gave evidence of lack of hygiene, facilities or care in the treatments used.

More damning evidence was given when James Cleary, who was manager of Smith and Sheppard Pharmaceutical Supplies of 95 Merrion Square, informed the court that he had sold a bottle of sea-tangle tents and two yards of rubber tubing to Nurse Cadden on 11 August 1943. The use of a sea-tangle tent in any operation other than a gynaecological one was hard to explain. Of the exhibits removed from the flat no sea-tangle tents were found, leaving the question to be asked as to what happened the ones purchased by Mamie just a year before.

In spite of the clarity of the evidence of Ellen Thompson there was something not quite right in it and the jury sensed it. Mamie did not treat people 'off the street'. She always insisted on a prior examination and a second appointment for treatment. This also increases the fees received by the practitioner. The idea of Ellen finding a two-year-old newspaper advertisement declaring 'male and female cases treated' and interpreting this as an advertisement for an abortion clinic was also hard to believe. Her evidence that Mamie didn't

even ask her for a down-payment before the operation does
not ring true either. Mamie did not give credit any more than
did her contemporary medical practitioners as betokened by
the two 'No credit given' signs in her flat.

This was the only one of the three trials that Mamie was
to go through in which there was direct evidence. There was
clear identification of Mamie as the person who examined
and operated on Ellen Thompson on 22 October 1944 and
the person who did the identification was Ellen Thompson
herself. Nevertheless even after such direct evidence the jury
took an hour and a half to reach a verdict of guilty as
charged. This was on Friday 27 April 1945. After the verdict
was delivered the judge rather gloatingly declared: 'If it is of
any interest to you I agree entirely with the verdict.' He also
stoutly defended the gardaí against allegations of misconduct
at the identity parade and against Inspector O'Neill in his
conduct of the case.

The sentence was handed down on the following Monday,
30 April 1945, the day Hitler committed suicide in his Berlin
bunker. Mamie was sentenced to five years penal servitude.
Judge Shannon said on passing sentence that he had treated
the case as an isolated one but that even so he had to impose
a sentence of penal servitude. This seems a remarkable statement considering the contents of Mamie's flat/clinic and can
hardly be anything other than purposeful self-deception at the
extent of abortion carried out in Dublin at the time. As for the
penal servitude element of the sentence it seems cruel now but
was certainly no more cruel that other sentences of the period.
The Dublin abortionists of the 1940s had been ruthlessly

stamped out. All got prison terms with penal servitude.

In a letter Mamie wrote in 1956 she makes some startling allegations.[47] She alleges that Larry Doyle, the husband of Ellen Thompson's employer, was in fact the father of the child Ellen was carrying and not some 'boy' as Ellen alleged in her evidence. If this was the case then it would certainly explain some glaring and unanswered questions relating to the case. How would a poorly paid maidservant pay for an expensive operation herself? Mamie alleges that Larry Doyle paid her £45, a sum impossible for a young woman working as a maid to accumulate. It also seems difficult to believe that a young woman with a sheltered upbringing like Ellen's would have been able to make an appointment by phone or in person and then go alone to keep this appointment. She would not have known where to go or what to do. Mamie had stopped advertising at this stage so established was her business. The story that Ellen gave that she was lighting the fire one day in her employer's house and when crumpling up a bit of a two-year-old newspaper saw an advertisement of Mamie Cadden's sounds a bit far-fetched. Finally the idea that a practical businesswoman like Mamie Cadden would do the operation on credit as Ellen alleges defies credibility.

The letter also alleges that Larry Doyle attempted to perform an abortion himself on Ellen Thompson with a piece of lead piping and a hat-pin which she claimed to have in her possession. There seems to be nothing available to support this remarkable allegation except perhaps the fact that Ellen did suffer from an infection that might have been caused by a third party. The evidence is too tenuous to make a decision in that direction and we do know that Mamie could be outrageous and nasty too. Now in her tribulations she turned savagely on her tormentors. If Larry Doyle had attempted such an operation then surely the last person he would have entrusted the instruments to would be Mamie Cadden.

By New Year 1945 large-scale abortion services in Ireland had been closed down by the combined efforts of the gardaí and the judiciary. The reporting by the Catholic hospitals of women with complications arising from abortions played a crucial role in identifying the women who would become the prosecution's main witnesses. It is hard to believe that there was anything other than a concerted movement to close down these facilities by the combined forces of Church and State. It is also quite remarkable that these facilities had existed in the new state almost without hindrance for the first twenty years of its existence.

Women of child-bearing age with no knowledge or access to contraception must now accept the possibility of conception after every sexual experience regardless of their consent. For many sexually active couples who would not practise abstinence this meant enormous families of sometimes over ten children; families of over twenty children were not unknown. Neither were women with health complications spared. Their duty was to put the life of the child they were carrying ahead of their own and thousands would carry their pregnancy to full term knowing it could mean their own death.

There was always the option of going to England for an abortion but it was far from easy. A government permit was required to travel to the United Kingdom until 1952 and anyway it was cumbersome and expensive.

The Dublin Central Criminal Court records catalogue the unspeakable horror of Ireland in the second half of the 1940s. They tell the stories of infanticide and child murder on an unbelievable scale. The perpetrators were almost always the children's mothers who must have been driven frantic with terror and fear at the idea of producing unwanted children. The poverty and the social stigma that drove them to such drastic acts were powerful indeed. In 1944 alone we have cases before the court of:

Norah Browne, Carlow, charged with murdering her
　　new-born baby boy;
Ellen Keogh charged with infanticide;
John Ennis, Meath, charged with murdering a newborn
　　infant;
Margaret Sommerville, Drogheda, charged with
　　manslaughter of a newborn child;
Joan Farrell, Kerry, charged with infanticide;
Mary Boylan, Leitrim, charged with the murder of an
　　unnamed male infant;
Catherine and Mary Walsh charged with the murder of a
　　child;
Margaret Holmes, Cork, charged with the murder of a
　　female infant.

Of the eight cases in the 1945 Dublin Central Criminal Court file for the first term of the year four related to the killing or attempted killing of children:

Elizabeth Rogers charged with the murder of her infant
   daughter;

Jane Battersby charged with attempting to drown,
   suffocate or strangle her child;

Briget Casey, Monkstown, was charged with the murder of
   her female infant;

William Henry Coleman charged on two counts with
   attempt to procure an abortion.

With so many cases coming to court, I think it is safe to
assume that many more were concealed. There is plenty of
anecdotal evidence available from district nurses and others
that many babies born at the period simply disappeared.

However we must go back to the files of 1943 to get a
focused picture. The file for this year contains twelve cases
for the Dublin Central Criminal Court. Is the pattern similar
to that for 1944 and 1945? One would certainly expect so.
However the 1943 file contains details of what one would
consider to be the more anticipated type of crime in a poor,
mainly rural society and not the predominantly child-killing
cases reflected in the 1944 and 1945 files.

Of twelve cases only one relates to the murder of a
newborn child. The only other case resembling the incidents
of 1944 and 1945 was the murder of a one-month-old baby
by Mary Kate Murtagh and Patrick McGough of Galway.

The conclusion may be drawn that the 1943–44 campaign
against the abortion clinics in Ireland extended to the widespread seeking out and charging of women on infanticide
charges in 1944 and 1945. These crimes existed in the 1920s

Mamie Cadden's prison photo of 1938 when first committed to Mountjoy Jail
Photograph © National Archives

198, *Mary O'Grady* 20. 7. 38

Molly (Mary) O'Grady: Mamie's assistant in the 1930s
and a co-defendent who was released after the 1944 trial
Photograph © National Archives

St Maelruin's, Mamie's nursing-home at 183 Lr Rathmines Rd

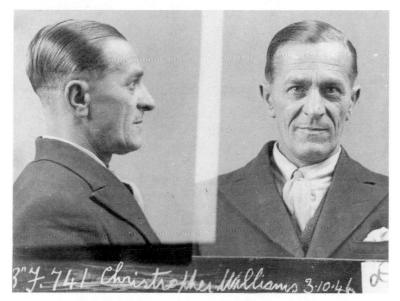

Christopher Williams: a chemist and Mary Moloney's partner.
They were jointly charged with procuring abortions
Photograph © National Archives

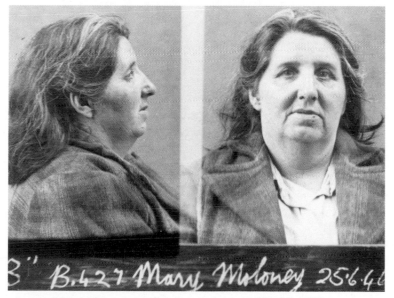

Mary Moloney: operated an abortion clinic with Christopher Williams
in Parkgate Street. She was sentenced to ten years penal servitude
Photograph © National Archives

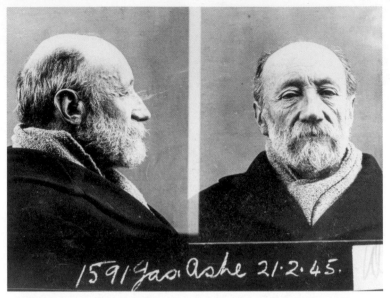

*Dr James Ashe: medical examiner to the matrimonial division of the high court. He was
jailed for abortion referral in 1945
Photograph © National Archives*

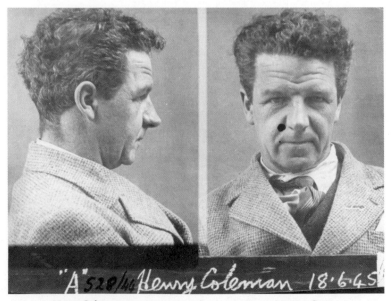

*Henry Coleman: ran an extensive abortion practice in Merrion Square
near the National Maternity Hospital in Holles Street in the 1940s
Photograph © National Archives*

No. 17 Hume Street where Mamie lived and worked until 1956
Photograph © National Archives

The chaotic inside of Mamie's Hume Street flat in 1956
Photograph © National Archives

Left: *Page from Mamie's diary for April 1956; the entry for April 17th had been clumsily changed from '8 p.m. Black Coat' to '2 p.m. Red Coat'*
Photograph © National Archives

Right: *The tragic and beautiful Helen O'Reilly*
who died in Mamie's flat on 17 April 1956
Photograph © National Archives

Stanley Siev, Mamie's solicitor in the 1956 trial

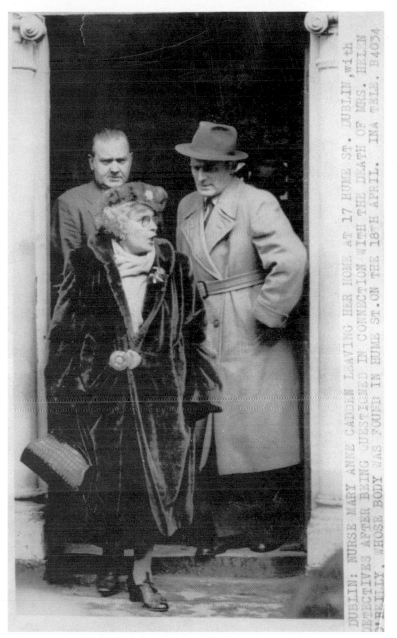

DUBLIN: NURSE MARY ANNE CADDEN LEAVING HER HOME AT 17 HUME ST. DUBLIN, with DETECTIVES AFTER BEING QUESTIONED IN CONNECTION WITH THE DEATH OF MRS. HELEN O'REILLY, WHOSE BODY WAS FOUND IN HUME ST. ON THE 18th APRIL. INA TELE. B4034

Mamie's arrest on 26 April 1956; she is accompanied by
Detectives Frank Moran (left) and Frank Carey (right)
Photograph © Atlantic Syndication

*The grave of Mamie's parents, Patrick and Mary, and of
her sisters, Ellie and Teresa, near their home in Lehardane, Co. Mayo*

*Deansgrave Cemetery: Mamie's final resting place, the mass grave for inmates of the
Criminal Lunatic Asylum in Dundrum. The headstone reads: 'Dundrum Mental
Hospital, Rest in Peace, Those Interred are not Named'*

and 1930s but not in the epidemic numbers of 1944 and 1945. It doesn't make sense to suggest that for some reason there was an unexplained outbreak of infanticide in 1944 and 1945. The truth may be the frightening thought that where contraceptive and abortion services are forbidden in society then infanticide increases dramatically. It was a horror story visited on the women and children of the state by its rulers.

On 30 April 1945, Mamie Cadden headed off to Mountjoy Jail to serve her second prison term. She was due for release on 29 April 1950. Her next of kin was entered as being her cousin, Patrick Martin, who lived in Fairview.[48] Her brother, Joseph, and sister, Eliza, were still alive but obviously estranged. Patrick Martin had testified at her trial and visited her shortly after she was jailed.

While in jail she was interviewed by her old adversaries, Superintendent O'Neill (formerly Inspector O'Neill), Detective Cryan and Detective King (formerly Sergeant King).[49] They were looking to see if Mamie would give evidence to incriminate the agents or doctors who had sent clients to her but that route was not for Mamie. With a bitter tongue and choice language she told them she was not an informer like Mary Moloney and Christopher Williams. They could go to hell! She'd serve her sentence, she told them, without any of their bloody favours – she was made of sterner stuff than that. Anyway, there was such a thing as professional confidentiality; she was a professional and her clients deserved and always were treated in confidence by her. During her long career she never once sought to share the blame or to implicate any of her accomplices even though to do so might have lessened the hostility of the gardaí to her and lessened the hardships of her prison terms. One can only imagine the abuse and invective she hurled at these men who had spent a large portion of their careers hunting down abortionists. They left without getting any information from Mamie.

She was soon back to her old self again and in April 1946 had fired her solicitor, Liam Trant McCarthy, and engaged Charles R. Phillips of 58 Merrion Square. The following year she was fighting with Phillips over the court exhibits that were entrusted to him. All were damaged, she alleged, and a ring was missing. Furthermore they were in a filthy condition. Whatever about the conditions in Mountjoy Jail and the severity of her sentence, Mamie Cadden's truculent spirit was not broken!

11

The Bleak 1950s

By the time that Mamie Cadden had served her second prison sentence Ireland had just entered the 1950s and the fourth decade of its independence from Britain. It was now called the Republic of Ireland but had achieved little in the way of prosperity, employment or civil liberties for its citizens. The regime in power now was called the Inter-Party Government (a coalition government composed of Fine Gael, Labour, National Labour, Clann na Poblachta, Clann na Talmhan and some independents) and was the first break from the Fianna Fáil government led by Éamon de Valera since 1932. John A. Costello, William Coleman's former defence lawyer, was now Taoiseach.

One might have expected that in its diversity the Inter-Party government would show a much more liberal face than its monolithic Fianna Fáil predecessor. However it was deeply infiltrated by members of the Knights of Columbanus, the secret Catholic organisation that aimed to promote Catholics to the higher positions in society and foster Catholic social policy. The two major leaders in this coalition were members: the Taoiseach and, surprisingly, the leader of the Labour party, William Norton.[50]

Initially the coalition was active and progressive but by 1951 had collapsed in a mess when Noel Browne, the young health minister, attempted to introduce a free health scheme for mothers and children. This offended the Catholic Church who considered it an intrusion into family life and the medical profession who considered it an intrusion into its professional area. There followed a massive Church/State confrontation and the Church, headed by the powerful Archbishop McQuaid, won a crushing victory. The government fell in 1951 as a result of this crisis and de Valera was returned to power.

In 1950 on her release from Mountjoy Jail Mamie entered her fifty-ninth year. The approach to sixty could hardly have been a happy time for one so proud of her appearance, image and material possessions. Her body was beginning to show the strains of her age and her six years spent in prison. Arthritis, no doubt exacerbated by her prison stay, and failing eyesight were starting to make life difficult for her. But she would not give in easily. She had always worked hard and would do so again. She rented a pokey little one-roomed flat at 17 Hume Street, off St Stephen's Green, not far from the fashionable Shelbourne Hotel where she could now drop in for a gin and tonic with the genteel customers in the Horseshoe Bar. The flat measured just eight feet by ten feet, hardly enough to swing a proverbial cat but she would continue working from it and hardly even needed to advertise. The room was tiny but it was in a very accessible location on some major bus routes. She had her own electric doorbell and more importantly her own telephone through which all her patients were expected to make an appointment before she would treat them. It was a far cry from her now palatial-seeming Victorian house in Rathmines or her extensive basement flat cum clinic in Pembroke Street but she would have to make do. All her contacts were still around and with the cowing of the medical establishment she would likely face a near monopoly situation on the abortion front.

There were formidable obstacles to be overcome. There was no running water in the flat and it had to be fetched in a bucket from an old-fashioned tap called a hopper, on the stairs. For Mamie Cadden, who had always adhered to the latest fashions and fads both in her private and professional life, it was another hard compromise to make. Now she was like her mother back in Mayo at the turn of the century, drawing water from the well. The flat was so small that there was no room for an examination table so any examinations had to be performed on the dining table. All her equipment and books of thirty years' medical practice were crammed in, making the room overcrowded and uncomfortable. She ate, washed, slept, examined and operated all in the same few square feet.

There were her physical problems too; she was at the beginning of a painful arthritic condition which affected her right hand and her right hip, both of which would get worse as the decade progressed. The condition of her hand was a serious problem making any manipulation, pulling or pushing with it painful indeed, quite a problem for examining and operating. There was also her eyesight, which was never strong. She had worn glasses since she was a young woman and her eyesight now deteriorated further with age. She wore strong glasses and these somewhat alleviated the condition.

Now approaching sixty with poorer facilities than she

ever had, with no one to help out, she who once employed a
staff had to start again on her own and with the added de-
bilities of approaching old age in a seedy bedsit in Hume
Street. After a while she became comfortable in this little
bedsit with pictures of dogs on the wall and a picture of
herself when she was young and beautiful. She settled down
and lost the desire to leave. Her great spirit now came into
play; she set up her business once again and, above all, kept
up appearances. Her hair was blonder than ever and soon she
was back in the Shelbourne Hotel bar downing her gin and
tonic, telling dirty jokes to the boys. She printed new business cards that included her own personal phone number.
The Dublin that had known her in her earlier years with her
big house in Rathmines and her open-topped MG sportscar
considered her the same glamorous Mamie. They did not
know the squalor behind the front door of 17 Hume Street
and Mamie would ensure that they never did. The reality was
known only to Mamie, her few friends – and clients, those
who shunned conventional medicine for her cures for dandruff, skin diseases and constipation. Above all, though, her
clients now were those unfortunate women and girls whose
pregnancies were so unbearable, dangerous or shameful to
them that they sought out Ireland's only well known abortionist, Mamie Cadden.

The authorities who moved so decisively against the abortion clinics in the early 1940s considered their work satisfac-
torily completed by 1946 with all the facilities closed and the
major protagonists in jail. By 1950 these were being released
but none showed the stomach to resume their former trade.

Indeed they probably did not have the resources either financial or physical to do so. Messrs Coleman, Flynn and McCabe would have spent massive amounts on their trials and appeals while Dr James Ashe would have been too old and infirm. Mamie Cadden, it appears, never gave the matter a second thought and commenced her work as soon as she could. One can only imagine the dismay her attitude caused but those in the know would have realised how small-scale her operations were in comparison to the situation in the 1930s or 1940s. From her small room in Hume Street she could have processed no more than a few clients each week adding up to a hundred or so a year or five hundred in the period of less than six years that she operated there.

She now got to know a new generation of Dubliners and Irish people in general, a generation brought up far from the liberal ethos of the 1920s when she had been in her prime. This new generation had been carefully brought up in the shadow of a very conservative Church in a very conservative state and sheltered from liberal and international influences. They knew her, they knew what she did and they left her alone. Boyfriends would taunt their girlfriends about 'having to go to Nurse Cadden' or 'if you carry on like that you'll soon be visiting Nurse Cadden'.

It was now June 1951 and Brigid Breslin was a dancer with the O'Dea/O'Donovan Troupe in the Olympia Theatre in Dame Street. She was thirty-three years old and lived the high life in so much as it could be lived in Dublin in the 1940s and 1950s. She was a beautiful, romantic and popular woman but most glamorous of all she was having an affair with a married man from County Cork: Standish O'Grady who lived at Carrigeen Hall, near Conna, Fermoy, which had once been an impressive mansion.[51] It now stood on 171 acres of prime farmland. Standish was a member of the old Anglo-Irish gentry, a dying breed in the new Irish state though he maintained all the airs and graces of a gentleman 'with means'. The money was almost gone but the pretensions remained. At one stage he had kept a racehorse called *Carrigeen* and he exhibited from his gardens in the RDS Spring Show. Like many of his class he had spent some time in the British armed forces, in his case in the Royal Navy. He rarely rose before noon and left the management of the farm to his staff. Nevertheless he was one of the old O'Grady family of Cork and Limerick with long and traceable pedigrees back to the Gaelic chiefs. Two of his relatives, both namesakes of his, Standish Hayes O'Grady and Standish James, had played major roles in the Celtic revival at the beginning of the twentieth century.

Standish met Brigid for the first time in the Parterre Bar of Cork Opera House when the dancers were on tour there in November 1950. On the very first night they headed off together for a few drinks in the Elm Tree Bar on the Cobh Road and their ill-fated relationship began. Standish was not one to hesitate when a beautiful girl was the prize. Poor Brigid must have really been swept off her feet. She must have thought that she had finally arrived: here she was driving through Cork in Standish's lovely grey Ford V8 car, and Standish was so handsome, so charming and so gentlemanly. He was practically an aristocrat; so rich with his posh accent and his house and servants near Fermoy. Not that it was straightforward for Standish; besides having a wife and family he already had another mistress, a nurse in a private hospital who had a flat in Ballsbridge where Standish stayed on the night of Brigid's death. His casual attitude to sex was to horrify the devout members of the gardaí. One of them was to write of him: 'He had no moral code regarding women.' Later on in June 1951 he would move his mistress into his Cork home as a nurse for his children when his wife was away in England for a holiday!

In the summer of 1951 disaster struck for Brigid; she discovered she was pregnant. Whatever about any other profession, pregnancy was not an option for a working dancer. Furthermore the troupe was due to go to England on an engagement and she wasn't about to miss it. Neither was marriage an option. Brigid lived in the working-class Buckingham Buildings in the north inner city far from the big gentry houses of north Cork. Besides the legal and religious prohibition on divorce and re-marriage there was a rigid social class-structure which would have forbidden such a liaison except for the most brave – and Standish was not one of those. Brigid wrote to Standish for help and he arrived up in Dublin on Thursday 8 June. They met in the Wicklow Lounge, part of the Wicklow Hotel just off Grafton Street and a well-known bohemian spot in Dublin that lasted right up to the 1970s. There they made arrangements for the following night.

On Friday evening Brigid was taken up to Nurse Cadden's flat by Standish O'Grady for an abortion. According to him it cost £20. The appointment was for 10.30 p.m. The method used was the pumping of a liquid into the womb through a special type of syringe called a Higginson syringe. It was a large enema type syringe that was fitted with a rubber tubing extension at the end and a nozzle that was inserted into the neck of the womb. The liquid was then forced out of the syringe and into the womb. This would separate the membranous bag containing the foetus from the wall of the womb. When this happens an abortion inevitably occurs. The liquid Mamie used was a mixture of water and the disinfectant Jeyes Fluid. The whole procedure required not only skill and dexterity but also a certain amount of strength and one can't help thinking of the arthritis in Mamie's right hand that must have surely made the procedure difficult for her. But things went horribly wrong on that night for Brigid Breslin. A pocket of air called an air embolism entered the blood system and travelled to her heart where it lodged in one of its chambers causing an interruption to the blood supply. Brigid was dead within minutes on Mamie's kitchen table.

Brigid's body was taken out to the street by Mamie, presumably with the assistance of Standish O'Grady. The body was discovered at 5.30 a.m. on Saturday morning on the footpath in Hume Street by a young medical student called Frank O'Neill who lived in the same house as Mamie.[52] He was returning home from a visit to a friend on the Navan Road when he met Gretta Harvey of Ely Place out walking her dog. Gretta had her own business, the Ely Ladder Mending Service, which repaired ladders in ladies' stockings. Probably because of the eyestrain caused by her work Gretta was a bit short-sighted. She saw a bundle on the street outside 19

Hume Street and asked Frank O'Neill, who was on the street at the same time, to check it out. Frank went up to it and found it to be the body of a dead woman. It was removed by fire brigade ambulance to the nearby Holles Street. The evening papers, the *Mail* and *Herald* hinted at the cause of death when they both reported that there were no external marks or injuries. On Sunday the state pathologist, Dr John Mc-Grath, performed a post-mortem examination.

The proximity of Mamie's flat to the location of Brigid's body was noted as was the fact that her death was the result of what was called 'an illegal operation' but nothing was ever proved, though a button from Brigid's dress was found outside Mamie's house by Garda Broderick. In Brigid's handbag was a letter with the O'Grady crest and the gardaí quickly concentrated their enquiries on this piece of evidence. They soon traced it to the Cork landowner. The gardaí approach to this case was humane and sensitive. They concentrated on the victim and on the person who made her pregnant and took her to the abortionist. The gardaí believed that this was Standish O'Grady but they were unable to bring any charges. Mamie was interviewed also but denied ever having met Brigid Breslin and there was no evidence against her. In quaint language the gardaí reported on the case of Brigid Breslin that 'No person was made amenable for her death'.

The Irish Times carried a report on the incident in the following Monday morning's edition. It reported that Brigid's relatives had been informed that death was due to natural causes. It also stated that she was coming from a party when she collapsed.

The death of Brigid Breslin was horrid and sad in itself but it also was to have serious consequences for Mamie Cadden. Though she was never charged as a result of the death or of any of the circumstances surrounding it, she was implicated nonetheless in people's minds. It gave rise to another urban myth concerning Mamie Cadden in which a picture was painted of the unfortunate woman lying bleeding in her lonely flat and dragging herself to Hume Street to the home of her abortionist for assistance, only to die on the street from loss of blood. This story was even put into print in the last decade of the twentieth century.

12

The Story of Helen O'Reilly

Mamie Cadden was now established in her tiny flat at 17 Hume Street. It was a house of flats owned by Laurence and Gertrude Brophy who lived at 24 South Great George's Street in the South City Hotel. Almost immediately Mamie and Gertrude were at daggers drawn. Mamie was never one to abide another strong woman especially one in a position of power over her as Gertrude was. The house was an extensive Georgian four-storey-over-basement house quite similar to the house in which Mamie had lived at 21 Pembroke Street during the 1940s. There were owner-occupiers in the vicinity and the area, though run down, was suffering only from the same shabbiness as most of the city in this economically depressed era. There were prosperous families in the area too: just round the corner the noted painter, Maurice MacGonigal, lived with his family in a house reserved for the keeper of the Royal Hibernian Academy; next door was 16 Hume Street, the headquarters of the Fine Gael party; and just across the street was the City of Dublin cancer hospital.

The entire house was let out in flats, Mamie occupied the back room on the first floor and the room at the front was occupied by an old woman, Mary Elizabeth Farrelly, who was the housekeeper at O'Neill's public house on Merrion Row. The basement flat was occupied by a Christopher O'Reilly, the ground floor flat called the hall flat was occupied by a Mr Flanagan, a commercial traveller, and his wife and son. The front second-floor flat held John O'Leary, a bookmaker, and his wife; and a Mr Noonan lived in the back flat. Michael Hogan, a retired bank official, lived in the top front bed-sitter, and the other top floor flat was occupied by John Moran, an unemployed baker, and his mother. The flat was rent-controlled which meant that the rent could not be raised except with the agreement of the court. In an era of atrocious housing conditions and shortages this was an attempt to keep rents at a reasonable level. It was a constant source of complaint by landlords who claimed it deprived them of the market value of the properties and of an incentive to improve them as this would be pointless when no higher rent could be charged. It was from here that Mamie conducted her medical business.

Abortion was still her main occupation but she never quite gave up on her other healing skills, treating dandruff, constipation and venereal disease, among others.

She had had a close escape in the case of Brigid Breslin and the gardaí were now watching her closely. One false step and she would be in deep trouble. As she passed the sixty-years mark she knew that she could never bear another term in jail and she had every intention of avoiding a charge. Standish O'Grady became a frequent visitor and enjoyed that rare status in Mamie's life of becoming her friend.[53] Sometimes he would bring patients to her by car, sometimes he would be around to drive them away. One woman relates how he answered the doorbell when she called for her dandruff treatment and waited round until she was finished.

From here, Mamie could have faded out; taking fewer patients as the years went by and she eased herself into old age. Towards the end of the 1960s Irish women were able to travel to Britain for abortions which became legal there in 1967 but in Ireland of the 1950s travel to Britain was difficult and abortion was still illegal. There was no avoiding it: 1950s Ireland still needed its abortionist.

The five years between 1951 and 1956 were to be difficult years for Mamie Cadden. In her miserable little bedsitter she endured the discomforts of reduced means: cramped surroundings and a lack of privacy which she had never endured outside of prison. Looking more like an old lady now, the glamour of her previous years was waning as her health and looks deteriorated. But she still kept up appearances and even though her bedsit was cramped it was still a lot better than Mountjoy Jail. Mamie was determined never to return there again and became very careful in her business. All appointments were made in advance, she took no business off the street and she never recorded names. It all worked remarkably well. The gardaí were frequent visitors and she knew that they were waiting for her first trip up to get her. It was during this period that she developed her real hatred of the gardaí. During her earlier days the invective that she'd thrown at them had something of the comic about it. Now an old lady she felt, with some justification, that they would hound her until her death. But true to form, Mamie would not take it without a fight and remarkably she was to remain ahead of the posse until 1956.

If any story were to be an example of one of the many tragedies of 1950s Ireland it would be the story of Helen O'Reilly. Hailing from Ballyragget in County Kilkenny, Helen Phelan was a remarkably beautiful woman with alluring, delicate looks, compounded no doubt by the fact that she had suffered from tuberculosis as a young woman. She had a tragic and vulnerable air yet she was a highly popular and extrovert woman who was the life and soul of the party or the pub.

The year after the war ended when Helen was in her early twenties she married John Francis O'Reilly, a classic ne'er-do-well whose family came from Tralee in County Kerry but settled later on in Kilkee, County Clare. His father had been a member of the RIC, the police force before Irish independence, and had participated in the arrest of Sir Roger Casement on Banna Strand at Easter 1916, an event which culminated in the hanging of Casement in the Tower of London. As a result of this, when the family moved to Clare they were known as the 'Casement O'Reillys'. Despite this background or maybe to rebel against it, John was a militant Republican who lost his civil service job in October 1938.[54] The file is still classified so one can presume that his dismissal was due to an intelligence report concerning his IRA activities.

When the Second World War started O'Reilly was working in the Channel Islands and when they were occupied by the Germans in 1940 he was taken to Berlin where he broadcast Nazi propaganda under the name of Pat O'Brien.[55] As if this weren't enough he was parachuted into Ireland on 16 December 1943 as an agent of the Abwehr, the German Secret Service. Like everything else he turned his hand to John

Francis wasn't much of a success as a spy. He landed near his father's home in Clare and was arrested within twenty-four hours! He was interned in Arbour Hill Prison in Dublin but escaped in July 1944 and made his way back to Clare to his father. His father promptly informed the gardaí of his son's whereabouts and then claimed and was awarded the reward money. When John O'Reilly was finally released from internment after the war his father gave him the money.

A little over a year after the war's end, on 24 November 1946, he married Helen Phelan. The newlyweds moved to Clifden in Galway and later to Dublin where John managed a small hotel near Kingsbridge Station. He turned his hand to a few different ventures, none of which was successful and eventually they ended up in rather poor circumstances in Bray, County Wicklow. By now Helen was just over thirty and had six children. In March 1955 John decided to bail out and got himself a job in Nigeria, then still a British colony, leaving his wife and six children behind; they had been married just eight and a half years. Helen, stuck in Ireland with no money, no job and six children must have faced a terrible dilemma. There was no welfare state to fall back on, the only benefit she would receive was children's allowance then paid in the father's name. Those who knew her say she was a very loving mother but what could she do? Even if she had a profession she could hardly work and look after six children and in any case economically depressed Ireland was not exactly awash with jobs at the time. All she could do was to fall back on the charitable institutions of the Church: the children were handed over to the nuns and distributed among various convents around Dublin. Helen headed for England. Her sister lived in Preston and Helen hoped she could make a fresh start there and maybe return later and collect her beloved children.

At great expense she returned frequently to Ireland to visit her children and was well known on the Dublin to Liverpool shipping line that left from Dublin's North Wall. According to James Beatty, a steward on the boat, the MV *Leinster*, she was a friendly and outgoing person. One of the children was looked after by the nuns in the Linden House in Blackrock and Helen was well known and popular with the staff. In Preston she was now experiencing the freedom denied to her when in Ireland looking after her six children. She frequented one of the local nightspots called the Ribble Club and her warm, outgoing character as well as her beauty made her a big hit with the men. It was here that she met James Wilson Byers with whom she had a relationship. It seems that Helen, deprived of a social life so long with constant childbearing and constant financial trouble was now going to make up for lost time.

In February 1956, almost a year after her desertion by her husband she suspected that she was pregnant. She went to Holles Street on 14 March on one of her visits to visit her children where she was examined by Dr Brian Hourihane. He confirmed that she was indeed pregnant. An appointment was made for her to return in about a month's time.

On 27 March she travelled back to Preston on the B & I boat and while on board she discussed her pregnancy with a man called Christy Fulton.[56] To his amazement she announc-

ed that she was going to get rid of it; it had been her intention all along. At thirty-three, with six children from her
marriage to John Francis O'Reilly, no present partner and
few prospects, the last thing she wanted was another pregnancy. She had even discussed a termination with two
friends, Kathleen Brown and Ann Sullivan. Anxious now to
end the pregnancy she purchased quinine tablets as abortifa-
cients, but whatever happened, her pregnancy continued –
quinine was not always successful as an abortifacient. It is a
bit of a mystery as to why she returned to Dublin for her
abortion, as there would have been plenty of abortionists in
England at the time but it may have been related to the
ending of her relationship with James Byers. Abortion was
still illegal in England but was widespread. Perhaps she felt
more at home and safer in Dublin, or perhaps the proximity
to her children made her feel more secure. Whatever the
reason she returned to Dublin on Thursday 5 April 1956.

Still extremely gregarious in spite of her crisis pregnancy,
she made friends on the boat with Herbert Doyle of Cabra
and travelled with him by bus from the North Wall where
the ship berthed. They travelled to Lower Abbey Street in
the centre of Dublin. Here they separated and she went to
meet a friend, Thomas Crowe, who had a flat at 21 Ely Place.
She stayed the night with him and left some of her belong-
ings with him in a leather holdall and a raffia bag. Just down
the road from his flat was the small room occupied by Mamie
Cadden from where she conducted her paramedical and
abortion service. This may explain Helen's thinking when
she decided to return to Dublin on this occasion.

From 7–12 April she moved into Cathleen Wood's boarding-house at 2 Buckingham Street, ironically very near where Brigid Breslin spent her last night. During that time she met an acquaintance in the Swiss Chalet, a café near the Shelbourne Hotel. The lady in question, who was involved with childcare, liked Helen and her children. She told Helen that if she didn't do something about the children that they might be taken away from her permanently by the authorities. Helen said that she intended taking them out of their institutions very shortly. On Friday night she was back with Thomas Crowe in his flat at 21 Ely Place. On the following day, Saturday, she met Patrick Hynes and spent the night with him in a boarding house in Westland Row. On Sunday she returned to Thomas Crowe's flat where hardly surprisingly she didn't get a great welcome and left shortly afterwards promising to return to pick up her things that still remained in his flat. Later on that day she called into Murray's Hotel in Marlborough Street where she met Joseph O'Gorman. She knew him of old and stayed with him that Sunday night in his flat in Leinster Road in Rathmines, not far from the house of Standish O'Grady. On Monday she spent the day going around the public houses in the city centre with Kathleen Harrison. We don't know where she spent that night. What must have been going on her head? What was she up to?

Tuesday 17 April was a fine spring day in Dublin and Helen set off for town wearing her smart black overcoat and carrying her red umbrella. She and a friend, Christina Keogh, started off the morning in flying fashion with a few drinks in

Dwyer's pub in Moore Street, the market area of Dublin. They stayed there until about 2.30 p.m. at which time the pub closed for a few hours. She took the short walk over to the Provincial Bank on O'Connell Street where she withdrew £15 from her account; the teller who served her was John Fletcher. After her visit to the bank Helen went down O'Connell Street to the Palace Restaurant near the bridge. There she ate a curry.[57] In the provincial backwater that was Dublin in 1956 it was the only restaurant in the city that served curry at lunchtime.

When the pubs re-opened at 4 p.m. she was back in again. This time it was Mooney's Pub in North Earl Street quite near to the bank and just off O'Connell Street. Here she had a few drinks more with another woman acquaintance, Bridget Meehan. Bridget left at about a quarter past five but Helen stayed on. She didn't leave until about half past six when she made her way over to O'Connell Street. In 1956 the focus for the street and the city's bus network was the Pillar, a nineteenth-century monument to Lord Horatio Nelson, the British naval hero and victor of Trafalgar, plonked right in the middle of O'Connell Street, on the site of the present Spire of Dublin. From here she got a No. 10 bus which travelled to Donnybrook in the city suburbs, through Dawson Street, St Stephen's Green, Merrion Row and Baggot Street. All these locations are near Hume Street and Nurse Cadden's flat. Helen, of course, knew the route well as it was the same one she would have taken many times to and from Thomas Crowe's flat in Ely Place. The nearest stop was in Merrion Row and she alighted here.

Shortly after 8 p.m. she stepped smartly up Hume Street, her red umbrella under one arm, handbag in the other hand. She wore a green and yellow outfit with a green beret. Covering it all was her smart black coat. She stopped for an instant outside No. 17 and then went up the four steps to the front door. With her gloved hand she pressed the doorbell that had 'Nurse' written on it. Helen O'Reilly had come to keep her appointment with Nurse Cadden for the abortion.

13

Mamie's Last Operation

Things were not going well for Mamie Cadden. She was not taking well to old age and reduced circumstances. Her temper, which was never the most placid seemed to be shorter nowadays as she struggled with arthritis, varicose veins and poor eyesight. Sometimes she spent most of the day in bed rising only to look after her few callers. Even though she didn't advertise anymore her reputation was enough nowadays to give her a few callers. The gardaí were watching her closely since Brigid Breslin's death and would be only too happy to pounce at her first mistake. It was Mamie against all of them. Oh for the good old days! Maybe better times would come. If only she could get this parasite of a landlord off her back. The landlords wanted to increase the rent or maybe to use an increase as a means of forcing out their notorious and increasingly difficult tenant. Whatever the reason there ensued a struggle between Mamie and her landlords, Gertrude and Laurence Brophy.

According to his wife, Laurence Brophy had ceased to collect the rent from Mamie because he claimed she had threatened him. The rent was now collected by his wife, Gertrude, who was by all accounts a much tougher character. Whether because they needed the money or that they wanted to get Mamie out of her small room, Gertrude Brophy now demanded an increased rent from Mamie. The increase was to be £4 a month, a substantial raise on a rent of about £15. There followed an altercation between Mamie and Gertrude that must have raised the roof. Mamie refused to pay; the rent had been fixed by law and she would not budge unless the law changed her rent. This may have appeared to Gertrude Brophy as a small matter of one awkward tenant refusing to pay an increase but to Mamie it was almost a life-and-death matter. Cooped up in her tiny room for most of the day and all of the night her future must have seemed bleak, and the sense of injustice at how she now eked out a living must have grated very sharply on her consciousness. No, she would not give in; she would not pay a penny more than the law demanded for this hovel. She would get Brophy and his pushy wife. Who did they think they were trying to push Mamie Cadden around!

On Monday, 16 April 1956, she wrote to the revenue commissioners about the Brophys and their attempted rent increase. She enclosed the receipts that she had and outlined some of her grievances including the failure of the Brophys to pay for the electricity as they had promised and the damaging of her nameplate and bell on the front door for which she also blamed her landlord. If she had left it at this then the story of Mamie Cadden might have been somewhat different but Mamie was not one for half-measures. She continued in the letter to outline the various injustices that had been meted out to her. She made charges against Larry Doyle, husband of Ellen Thompson's employer, of attempting to perform a do-it-yourself abortion on her with a piece of lead piping and a hat-pin in 1944. She also accused a local priest, Fr Boylan, of having a sexual relationship with the mother of the child that was dumped near Dunshaughlin back in 1938. She also made some other quite substantial allegations that were lost in the hysterical and accusatory tone of the letter.

Mamie was in serious trouble and she knew it. Here she was, an old woman now, cornered at last and aware that Gertrude Brophy would probably win. If it went to court Brophy could fight again and again to have the rent increased. Her frustration boiled over and, as she would often describe her own temper tantrums, she was 'in flames'. It was what she put at the end of the letter that really landed her in trouble. It was something that she often said but had not before committed to paper. At the very end of her letter, almost as an afterthought she wrote about her tormentor: 'Irish Landlords. If he comes in here to put me out, I will shoot him dead and also put the butcher knife to the handle in his pot belly.' It was no more than her father would have said fifty years previously about his landlords, the Gores or their land agent. She sent the letter by registered post to the revenue commissioners.

She wasn't prepared for what happened next. One step ahead of her the Brophys acted immediately and on Tuesday Mamie received an official letter regarding her tenancy demanding that she vacate her flat. It was a legal document entitled 'Notice to Quit'.[58] Mamie was flabbergasted. How could this have happened? It couldn't be real; it must be a forgery. That was it, the Brophys had sent her a fake notice. This could not be an official document, it couldn't be genuine. She asked Mick McAuley to look at the document to see if it was genuine. Mick was a friendly parking attendant on Hume Street who Mamie often invited to her flat for a chat and a cup of tea. She knew from his reaction that he thought it was. He advised her to consult a solicitor. She swore vengeance against Laurence Brophy. She would fix him, she said, for trying to put her out on the street. He'd do it over her dead body, she swore. When Mick left she was still in a temper.

She lay on the bed for a while trying to calm down. She had better pull herself together, she thought, she had an appointment later on in the evening. It would be a hard one, a married woman with an unwanted pregnancy who was five months gone – but they were all fecking hard these days with her arthritic wrist. She wasn't in the form for it tonight though, not after that letter. She didn't even feel great. Nevertheless she had accepted the business and she could do with the money. So Mamie Cadden put her feet up and lay on the bed while she listened to Radio Eireann. Her client was due to arrive at 8 p.m. She had put her into her appointments diary according to the coat she had worn when she had made the arrangement: it read '8.00p.m. Black Coat'.

The doorbell rang shortly after the 8 o'clock time scheduled for the appointment but for once Mamie didn't mind. The break had given her time to pull herself together and to recover from the implications of her chat with Mick McAuley. She would have to find a new solicitor in the morning. If Gertrude and Laurence Brophy were going to shift her they wouldn't do so without a fight. My God, how she hated the prospect of looking for a new flat and all the prissy tight-arsed, stuck-up landladies of Dublin looking down at her through their noses – she who could once have bought and sold them. Now she would have to go to them like a young nurse from the country seeking their approval to pay an exorbitant rent for some dive. It just wasn't bloody fair. It was in this frame of mind that she walked Helen O'Reilly up the stairs to her room on the first floor landing. Wrapped in her red dressing-gown that she had worn all day she re-entered her room and Helen removed her black overcoat and her silk headscarf.

Helen could sense Mamie's hostility and had no way of knowing that it was not aimed at her. She'd get out of here as quickly as possible after the operation, buy a Baby Powers or even a naggin in O'Donoghue's of Merrion Row and go to bed. Tomorrow it would all seem like a bad dream and she would go to see her children. She handed over the £15 for the operation to Mamie. It was an awful amount of money but worth it, she supposed, to have someone as professional as Mamie Cadden. She might be an unpleasant old witch but she was very good at what she did. Everyone said that, all her lady friends swore by her and many of them had reason to know.

Mamie's flat was dreadful and cluttered. How could anyone live here Helen wondered? She didn't even have a water tap in the flat and had to go out to the landing to fill some water into the enamel bucket. Into the water Mamie put some Jeyes Fluid making a pungent smell. Helen could only think of hospitals when she got a whiff of this; she knew what was coming next. She lay on the table, closed her eyes and clenched her fists as the nozzle from the big syringe now full of the disinfectant solution was inserted by Mamie into her. Mamie was very careful and it didn't hurt much but the feeling of intrusion was horrible. It was very undignified and unladylike. Now she felt something move inside her, it kept going on and on, this was it she thought, this was the operation. Then she felt a sharp stab of pain and was sure that too was part of the procedure; but it wasn't. She opened her eyes and looked up in a desperate and frightened sort of way. Her last sight was of Mamie Cadden now panting slightly, a grimace of pain on her face as she tried to expel all the liquid from the syringe.

Mamie began to panic. She hadn't had enough strength to push the solution from the syringe into the womb in one go. Her wrist was hurting like hell. She just couldn't do it. She'd had to stop in the middle of it. That's when it happened, she must have retracted the plunger on the syringe ever so slightly so that when she pushed it in again a small air bubble was pumped into the womb. The air enters the blood supply through the membranous bag holding the foetus that she was in the process of dislodging from the wall of the womb. That was it, she thought; straight to the heart, immediate interruption to the blood supply and the poor bitch is dead, dead as a doornail. Dead on my table. What the hell am I going to do now? It's all the fault of that bloody cow, Gertrude Brophy; if she had left me alone I would have done all right. I can't bring her out on the street. I wouldn't be able to carry her anyway. I wouldn't have the strength to do it and even if I could I'd have the whole house out on the landing with the racket. I can't keep her here and I can't get rid of her. Oh my God, what will I do?

Mamie just stood there in the middle of her tiny room staring at the warm, partially undressed body of Helen O'Reilly. She sat down on the bed, her jaw slightly open as the shock set in. 'I'm not taking the rap for this,' she said out loud. She went through the list of people she knew who could help her. Mamie Cadden, now in her sixties, suffered the indignity of needing help – she who had scorned all offers of help for forty years. She couldn't do this alone; she just didn't have the physical strength. She needed a man. God it was pathetic, at this stage of her life that she needed a man. There was only one person for the job, only one person that wouldn't get all hysterical and squeamish on her, one person who owed her a great deal: Standish O'Grady. He lived in Leinster Road West but he drove a motor car. Perhaps he would take the body away, get her out of the premises. She could hardly leave her on the street. After Brigid Breslin that would be just inviting trouble. Yes, Standish was the man. Everyone knew he was connected with Brigid Breslin but she had kept her mouth shut and no one was able to prove anything. Now perhaps she could have the same luck with Helen O'Reilly.

She telephoned Standish and told him it was an emergency: 'Could you come over as quickly as possible? ... No, I'll let you know when you arrive.' She couldn't tell him over the phone what the matter was; you'd never know who was listening. Anyway, she knew that this would make him come more quickly as he was a real gossipmonger. It was now almost 9 p.m. and she was sitting in the room with the corpse of Helen O'Reilly. She made tea for herself. 'Bloody hell!' she thought, 'this is a real mess. How am I going to get myself out of this one?' She turned on the radio again. She couldn't bring herself to touch Helen O'Reilly who was still stretched out on the table. 'Oh Standish,' she implored, 'Get here quickly.' She didn't have to wait long. At about twenty past nine the doorbell rang. She wrapped the red dressing-gown tightly around herself and went downstairs to let him in.

She took him into the big hallway just inside the front door. 'Can't I come up?' he asked in his slightly posh drawl.

'No, you bloody well can't, and you wouldn't want to if you saw what I have on the kitchen table.' Mamie chuckled slightly as she delivered these lines and looked straight into Standish's eyes.

'Oh God, not again?' he groaned.

She took a sharp intake of breath: 'Don't come all moral on me now, Standish O'Grady. You know that these things happen, I took every precaution and you know I did. It was the same as with that unfortunate bitch, Brigid Breslin. An air embolism: air trapped in the bloodstream that went straight to the heart. I have to get rid of the body.'

'What do you expect me to do, take it home with me to Lillian? Mamie, I just can't help you on this one. They're watching me too. They know all about my affair with Brigid, they'd hang me for this.'

'They'd hang me too, or put me back in Mountjoy which would be the same thing anyway. I'm finished, Standish, if you don't help me on this one. You're the only one I can depend on.'

It was true. She knew Standish was a gentleman. For all his shabby gentility and notions of grandeur he would not let a lady down. Not that he was much use really in planning a thing – she would have to do all that but at least he had the physical strength to get the body out without waking up the whole house. She couldn't even do that on her own with the bloody arthritis, dammit! It had turned her into a useless bag of aching bones.

Standish was very reluctant but having shown up in response to her urgent summons he felt that he couldn't get out of it now. But he wouldn't take her away in his car. He drew the line at that. He wouldn't have her in the car at all. He'd help Mamie shift her out on to the street. That was all; he wouldn't do anything else. He stayed in the hallway talking to Mamie until about 11 p.m. and then moved out on to the steps in front of the house. God, she was persuasive but he couldn't let her down – not now that her back was against the wall. He was rather fond of the old battleaxe anyway. Her bark was worse than her bite and she was the only one who had a sense of humour in this bloody awful city. He'd help her all right but on his terms. He was a well-known person; he didn't want to get mixed up in what could well become a murder investigation.

While they were talking in the hallway three people from the house walked past and when they went outside the front door other people passed by on the street. One was Muiris MacGonigal, the fourteen-year-old son of the painter and keeper of the Royal Hibernian Academy. He knew Mamie well and was often in the house playing with the Flanagan boy in the hall flat. He was very fond of Mamie and they often spoke together. She knew about paintings and had some Irish, things that were very important in his house. She was constantly encouraging him to work hard and make something of his life.

So Standish made the arrangements with Mamie. He would return at six o'clock in the morning exactly and then he would help her take the body out and leave it on the path. Then it would be in the hands of providence and if past times were anything to go by then they could pin nothing on Mamie and she would get away with it as she had done previously. Mamie was not too enamoured with his plan but it wasn't as if she was calling the shots. For once Standish felt he had the upper hand on Mamie. With this he turned, walked down the steps and over to his car which he had parked a little way from the house, on St Stephen's Green. Mamie retraced her steps up to her flat, now the eerie receptacle of the body of Helen O'Reilly. Mamie covered the body with her own black coat and slipped into the bed, apparently unperturbed by the presence of the corpse within hand's reach.

At five to six she was waiting just inside the front door so that when Standish arrived at five minutes past she was able to open the front door for him when he tapped lightly on it. Helen O'Reilly was a slim woman, no more than nine stone, and Standish and herself were well able to get her down the stairs without too much bother. Mamie jammed the front door open, took a quick look up and down the street and when she saw that the coast was clear they moved out. Once outside they turned left and down past No. 16. At No. 15

they stopped, totally out of breath and strength. They left down the body and Standish raised his hand and waved to Mamie without saying a word. He then walked briskly around the corner to where his car was parked on Ely Place.

Mamie looked down at the body of Helen O'Reilly and, not satisfied that she was far enough away from No. 17, dragged her a few yards further until she was at the far side of No. 15 and beside the steps leading down to its basement. She breathed a sigh of relief. She quickly walked back into her own house and made up a parcel containing Helen's shoes, handbag and a macintosh she had been carrying. She also took her umbrella and overcoat. She dropped the parcel on the basement steps and threw the umbrella down after them. She covered the body with the overcoat and then retreated back into the house as quickly as she could. Once inside the security of her little flat she flopped into her chair, her heart beating so loudly she thought it might burst.

14

Discovery

Hume Street was no longer a focus of nocturnal activity as it had been in the 1920s and even up to the start of the 1950s when the ladies of the night met their clients or entertained them in the basements there.[59] Now in this depressed city Hume Street had acquired a somewhat more dignified air with the cancer hospital just opposite Mamie's flat and the Fine Gael party headquarters next door; they lent a sedate tone to the small street. At the very end of the street was the headquarters of the Knights of Columbanus and a few doors up from No. 17, Opus Dei, another secretive Catholic organisation, was to set up its information centre and hostel. Mamie certainly had some incongruous neighbours.

Hume Street, nonetheless, did have its night-time and early morning urban life, as newspaper deliverers, milk-float drivers and early morning workers traversed the street. Mary Galvin who lived at No. 15 where the body was found returned home by taxi at around 3.40 a.m. She saw nothing on the street nor did her driver. Hume Street was then lit by gas with the individual lights extinguished manually. The gasman was Martin Byrne and among the other lights he quenched was the one outside No. 15. The lamp was just where Helen's body was found but Byrne saw nothing. This was at 4.45 a.m.

Patrick Gleeson was a milk deliveryman for the Tel-el-Kebir dairy in Monkstown. He arrived in Hume Street at about 5.05 a.m. to make his usual delivery to the cancer hospital. As he got out of his lorry he said he saw what he thought was a bundle of clothes on the other side of the road where the body was later found. He didn't go over to examine the bundle as he was running late. He left at about 5.30 a.m. while it was still quite dark; the bundle was still there. Next to arrive was Nicholas Ellis who was the driver of the *Irish Independent* delivery van; he saw nothing and neither did his helper, John Walsh. This was at 5.40 a.m., at least ten minutes after Patrick Gleeson said he saw the 'bundle'. At about the same time Nurse Mary Fitzgerald looked out of the hospital and saw nothing. These two witnesses sow some seeds of doubt as to the testimony of Patrick Gleeson. John Harding of Oliver Bond Flats, a newspaper deliveryman for *The Irish Times*, dropped a paper at 9 Hume Street at 6.30 a.m. and he saw nothing but he wouldn't have had a great vantage point.

The key evidence of discovery and the person remembered as the finder of the body in Hume Street is Patrick Rigney of Colepark Drive, Ballyfermot, a new suburb of Dublin.[60] He was a milk roundsman employed by Lucan Dairies Ltd. Yet his story is strangely inconsistent and changed significantly in the course of the trial. It is difficult to know if he was currying favour or attention, or if his memory was playing tricks on him as the trial progressed – or indeed if the excuse he put forward himself for changing his testimony was true. Whichever was the case, he was to cause great damage to Mamie Cadden's defence.

He said that when driving down St Stephen's Green at 6.20 a.m. he looked up Hume Street which was at right angles to his route and saw a bundle on the path. Later on he was to say that he saw a woman stooping over the bundle and he described her in detail, something entirely questionable given the tiny period he had to look as his vehicle moved on. Next he said he doubled back and drove up Hume Street, stopping outside No. 11 and getting his helper Anthony Kiernan to make the delivery there. Rigney got out of his van and saw that the bundle was indeed the body of a woman partially covered by a black coat. Later he was to change his story and to say that he then heard a noise from the basement area in front of the house and took a few steps forward and looked down. There he saw a woman looking back up at him. He said that she had glasses and fair hair 'puffed out in front'. Though he never identified her as Mamie Cadden the description he gave was enough. Blonde hair and glasses were always enough to identify Mamie in the Ireland of the period. Rigney then said that he continued his deliveries up in Ely Place where he met another roundsman, Patrick McCarthy, from Dublin Dairies and had a short conversation with him. Surely very strange behaviour for someone who had just discovered a body and a potential key witness.

Anthony Kiernan, his helper, was strangely reticent in his story of that morning but contradicted his boss on only one point. After Ely Place they did not go on to Baggot Street initially, as Rigney was to say, but doubled back, up Hume Street and down St Stephen's Green where they would have

driven to Baggot Street via Merrion Row. This was important evidence as it meant they would have passed the body
and perhaps the woman Rigney saw yet again. It was the only
evidence that the young helper gave that challenged his
boss' version. When they reached Baggot Street Rigney reported the matter to Garda Timothy Fallon who was in the
area and who made his way up to Hume Street and reached
there at 6.32 a.m. There he found the body of Helen O'Reilly
lying on the pavement outside No. 15 Hume Street.

Poor Helen, always so graceful, so careful about her
appearance lay sprawled in the most undignified fashion on
the footpath. She lay in front of the railings of No. 15 by the
gate leading down into the basement. Her legs projected
slightly through the gateway and over the stone steps that
led down to the basement. Her head faced back towards St
Stephen's Green and No. 17 Hume Street. She was covered
by her black overcoat but under this were her green and
yellow jacket and matching skirt which were over her head.
On the skirt was pinned her green beret. Her white petticoat
was up around the middle of her body and her corset was
turned up also. A piece of net cloth and her torn knickers
were tied around her legs above the knees and were secured
with a large safety pin. Her scarf and a stocking were loosely
tied with a bow-knot around her neck. One of her stockings
was down around her ankle and the other was up about three
inches above her knee. It was obvious from the disarray of
her clothes and the dirt marks on them that she had been
dragged for the final small distance. She also wore her wed-
ding and engagement ring, earrings and a cross and chain

On the footpath behind her was a mark going back about three feet that would suggest that she had been dragged only that distance.[61]

Garda Fallon walked across the road to the cancer hospital where he asked for someone to come over to examine the body. Nurse Katherine Doyle was on duty and immediately went over. She was satisfied that Helen was dead. In fact when she tried to raise the left arm there was an amount of stiffness: rigor mortis was already setting in. Another guard, Pat Carmody, arrived on the scene and Garda Fallon left to inform his superiors in the Harcourt Terrace garda station about what had happened. Immediately the top brass realised that they had the highest profile case of their careers on their hands; their chance to catch and nail Mamie Cadden, the constant thorn in their sides. By ten past seven that morning the site outside No. 15 Hume Street was a *Who's Who* of Dublin gardaí: Chief Superintendent Farrell, along with Superintendent Moran, Inspectors Scanlon, O'Connor and O'Grady, Garda Detectives Scally and Lang and Sergeant Simon Finucane. Father Vincent Lee administered the last rites to Helen. The scene was cordoned off and a crowd started to assemble. It soon became vociferous and hostile. The mob knew who they wanted for vengeance. At about 8.10 a.m. Mamie's curiosity got the better of her and she stuck her head outside the door of 17 Hume Street and then walked out onto the steps.[62] As soon as they saw her, the crowd howled and hissed in accusation with shouts of 'There she is! There's the murderer! There's Cadden.' Mamie looked blankly at them and went back inside.

Dr Maurice Hickey, the state pathologist, arrived at the scene at 8.20 a.m. and ascertained the temperature of the body as 29°C, the normal temperature of a living person being 37°C. The air temperature he calculated was 18°C, a suspiciously high reading indeed given that the month was just April and it was still morning. Temperature was later to feature in the trial. Official gardaí photos were taken and the body was removed by hearse to the city morgue in Store Street under Dr Hickey's supervision. The contents of her handbag showed quite clearly who the deceased was as among its contents was her bank book but a formal identification was still necessary. Helen's brother-in-law, Michael McSwiney, of New Ireland Road, Rialto, performed this sad task at 4.30 in the afternoon.

Dr Maurice Hickey had completed the post-mortem by 11.15 a.m. on the same day.[63] He flooded the chest to examine the heart underwater and found that the right chamber was distended and fraught. When he opened the heart a considerable amount of air bubbled out. He also opened the great vein in the abdomen under similar circumstances and again found the presence of air. The womb was enlarged by the presence of a pregnancy of a male child of about five months. The membranous bag that contained the foetus was not damaged. However it was separated from two-thirds of the back and left-hand side of the wall of the womb as was part of the afterbirth. This separation was not natural. The separated surface of the membranous bag had a rough, shaggy appearance indicating that it had been forcibly torn from the wall of the womb. He noticed a distinct smell of some sort of disinfectant or antiseptic coming from the wall of the womb in this region. He found a minor degree of inactive tubercular disease of old standing at the top of both lungs. He also found a build up of fat in the liver as is common during pregnancy.

He concluded that the cause of death was heart failure due to an air embolism. By this he meant an interruption of the blood stream by the presence of a quantity of air which in this case was lodged in the chambers of the right hand side of the heart. There it had formed a froth which had resulted in the stoppage of the circulation of the blood. The air had entered through the blood vessels of the afterbirth at the point where it had been separated from the wall of the womb. He gave his opinion that the fatal entry of air into the circulation system could not have occurred naturally. He concluded that it resulted from an injection of some substance between the membranous bag and the wall of the womb. In this case that substance was a watery fluid containing some antiseptic or disinfectant. To accomplish this, he believed, some instrument of a tubular nature must have been used and inserted through the neck of the womb.

He found very little bleeding and no damage to the womb or the neck of the womb. This, he declared, would require some skill. His conclusion therefore was that the person who performed the operation was a person of 'some skill' in this area. Though it was a compliment of sorts for Mamie Cadden it was to be damning evidence. From the body temperature he estimated the time of death to between 2 a.m. and 3 a.m. if the death had occurred where the body had been found and left there. If however, the body had been left in a warm room until between 5 a.m. and 6 a.m. and then placed in Hume Street, he estimated the time of death as being much earlier depending on the temperature and humidity of the room. Assuming the body to have been covered then he would have put the probably time of death as between 9 p.m. and midnight of the previous night.

An important finding was that there was no skin damage to the neck which disproved the allegation that Helen O'Reilly was pulled down the street by the stocking tied around her neck. In fact, Helen was facing the other way round making it obvious that she was taken down Hume Street feet first. Dr Hickey also found some traces of the curry which Helen had eaten at lunchtime when he examined her digestive system.

After the indignity of the post-mortem Helen O'Reilly was buried in Glasnevin Cemetery on Dublin's northside. Even now the cruelty of her life was compounded. She was buried under the Irish version of her name. It is a language of which she would have had little or no knowledge owing to her lack of schooling and indicated a final disowning by her husband who had returned from Nigeria for the funeral of the mother of his six children.

Shortly after Mamie had stuck her nose out on the street to see what was going on, two gardaí, egged on by the crowd, went up to her doorstep and rang the bell. It was 8.15 a.m. and Detective Gardaí Sullivan and Scally were rather quick off the mark. The door was answered by a co-operative Mamie still in her red dressing-gown. She even asked them in and they accompanied her up to her little flat. There, in the middle of the floor, was an enamel bucket with some greyish/-brownish liquid in it that they thought was diluted Jeyes Fluid. Detective Garda Sullivan asked her if she had heard anything unusual during the night or early morning and Mamie replied that she hadn't. She went on to explain that her room was at the back of the building and that she had the radio on all night for company as she was unable to sleep with her arthritis. She also showed them her legs which were heavily bandaged to relieve the pain from her varicose veins. When they told her that the body of a young woman had been found outside No. 15 she replied: 'God help us. Sure it must have been a man that did that.'[64] While they were in the room the phone rang. They identified the caller as male but Mamie did not address him by name. It seems likely that it was Standish O'Grady telephoning to find out if the body had been found. Mamie kept repeating 'Yes' down the line to tip him off that she was not alone and she even went so far as to say, 'Yes, yes I'll do that for you', before she could get the clueless Standish off the line.

These two gardaí were only the advance guard of what was to descend on her later in the afternoon by which time Mamie had taken a few precautions. Years later two boxes of medical instruments were found in her elderly neighbour's adjoining flat by students living in the house. The neighbour was Mrs Farrelly who was later to give damaging evidence against Mamie so it's unlikely that she cooperated in the hiding of the instruments. It's more likely that Mamie used one of Mrs Farrelly's absences from her flat to hide the two boxes there without her knowledge. Mamie had a busy morning and afternoon. At 3.45 p.m. Superintendent Moran and other officers, armed with a search warrant, called back to Mamie's flat. She was quite co-operative and told them to 'Search away'. Moran found some medical instruments and removed them for examination. They included a new Higginson syringe, which is a large enema-type syringe, a surgical forceps, a flushing curette (a spoon shaped instrument which can be used for removing tissue from a bodily cavity) and two duck-billed specula. Nurse Cadden was quite unperturbed by the finds and said that she had the specula since her time in the nursing-home in Rathmines and that she used the forceps as a tongs for the fire. Detective Sergeant Martin took Mamie's diary and her red dressing-gown.

The facts of the matter were that the gardaí had no evidence whatever to connect Mamie Cadden with the death of Helen O'Reilly. Nobody came forward to give evidence that the two had ever met. Helen was not seen entering 17 Hume Street and it was not until later that Patrick Rigney changed his evidence to indicate that he had seen a woman near the body making this part of his evidence suspect. At this stage public hysteria had reached fever pitch. Every pub in Dublin and every conversation in Ireland had condemned Mamie Cadden as the abortionist. 17 Hume Street became the most visited site in Ireland with crowds assembling each day to visit the scene of Helen O'Reilly's death and to perhaps catch a sight of Mamie Cadden, now cast in the role of Ireland's evil woman.

If Mamie cared about the venom with which she was now treated she gave no indication of it. Outwardly she was full of brazen bluster and contempt for her tormentors. If the gardaí couldn't nail her then the mob would move off to find some other victim.

'Feck them all!' was her only response.

She had a point. The gardaí had no evidence against her. Their interviews with the other tenants in the house were inconclusive and could hardly sustain a charge. But they were intent on not being thwarted on this occasion. The approach to the case was to be fundamentally different to the approach to the Brigid Breslin case in 1951. Now the concentration was to be on convicting Mamie Cadden as the mob demanded. If there were no witnesses available then the technical evidence must suffice and surely in this modern age they could prove the presence of Helen O'Reilly in Mamie's room on the night of 17 April. If they could do that then the jury would surely convict. This was the only course available to them.

It was now all over to the garda technical bureau, headed by Superintendent George Lawlor. Lawlor made the arrest of Mamie Cadden a personal crusade. He was obsessed with her conviction. 'This is a breaking of minds,' he said, 'and I'm going to break Cadden.'[65] The only way this could now be done was through the presentation of a body of technical evidence. A huge and expensive technical investigation, the most extensive in the history of the state now took place, all aimed at the conviction of Mamie Cadden. But Mamie stood her ground.

15

The Witch-Hunting of Mamie Cadden

It was all circumstantial. Nobody had seen Helen O'Reilly on Hume Street, let alone entering No. 17. She had never been seen in the company of Mamie Cadden. In Mamie's diary they found two entries for 'Black Coat' and as one of these, the entry on the night of Helen's death, had been tampered with and changed to 'Red Coat', they took it as code for Helen O'Reilly. The gardaí felt their suspicions were confirmed but it was rather flimsy evidence. A desperate search began for dust particles, blood traces, fibres or hairs on Helen's body and clothing to connect her with the inside of Mamie's flat. The gardaí were unused to such minute and painstaking work. It was their first major adventure into the world of the technical, forensic evidence that was to play such a major part in the court presentations of the rest of the century.

Meanwhile Mamie sat in her flat giving interviews to the newspapermen who visited her; telling lewd stories about the gardaí and posing for photographs. She entertained her visitors as much as she infuriated the gardaí who felt powerless in the face of a case which was rapidly going nowhere. A young journalist from *The Irish Times* visited her named Cathal O'Shannon, who was later to make a name for himself as a television broadcaster. She told him that the gardaí had called and had taken away some matting and a pair of

duck-billed specula. 'Do you know what they're for?' she
asked the journalist. When he replied that he didn't she said,
'They're for looking up a whore's flu,' and cackled with
laughter. She spoke to a *Daily Express* reporter of the hatred
that the mob had for her: 'People in Dublin always hated me
because I had so much money,' she said defiantly, adding that
she made her money from 'a secret hair restorer'.

Whatever about the mirth inside the flat, outside was the
mob, shouting for Mamie's blood. Such an outcry had not
been seen since the foundation of the state. It was witch-
hunt hysteria.

The gardaí returned to see Mamie eight days after the
body was found on Thursday 26 April. She was cautioned by
Superintendent George Lawlor who then rather theatrically
produced the forceps, the Higginson syringe and the diary, all
of which had been seized from her the previous week. She
acknowledged ownership and said that she had never used
any of them for any surgical reason since she had left her
nursing-home in Rathmines. She made a new statement and
explained what her work was: 'I deal with hair trouble, duodenal ulcers and varicose veins. I also give enemas. As a matter of fact, in the case of duodenal ulcers I have to give
enemas in all cases as they come from the one source: constipation.' He questioned her about the entry in her diary on
30 March reading '£50'. This would have seemed too much
for any treatment such as she outlined, like dandruff or
constipation. But Mamie was not to be outsmarted. This
charge, she alleged, was for professional services for a family
of two or three.

He questioned her extensively about the man with whom she talked for almost two hours in the hallway and outside the front door. We now know this man as Standish O'Grady from witnesses who later identified him but in a remarkable show of loyalty Mamie insisted that the man in the hall was 'from the country' and that he had called for treatment for his arthritis. At first she thought she would give him the cortisone – with which she treated the condition – but then decided that she was too tired as he had arrived so late. She would not give his name as she would not drag him 'into the dirt'. He had travelled from 75 to 200 miles to see her.[66] Bluffing his way shamelessly Lawlor told her that he had information that Helen O'Reilly was in Nurse Cadden's room on 17 April and that she was wearing a black coat. He had no such information as he presented none at the trial.

She also made a famous and much repeated remark about the unfortunate Helen O'Reilly. It seemed as if it was almost designed to lose her sympathy. Mamie was often scathing about her clients particularly about her women clients and now she surpassed herself, referring to a photo of Helen O'Reilly on the previous day's papers: 'I took up the *Evening Mail* of 25 April,' she said to Superintendent Lawlor, 'and I passed a remark to a man who was here, that she had the mouth of a prostitute.' They searched the tiny flat again and this time took five of Mamie's combs, an enamel douche can, two electric lamps and a large safety pin. At this stage it was clear that they were building up a case from scratch and that they had nothing new on the previous week. They left and Mamie must have breathed a sigh of relief. She posed for a photograph from Fennel's photographers and perhaps laughed at the way the gardaí had been foxed again.

Her illusions were shattered however when, within the hour, the gardaí returned again. Her rights were read to her and she was charged, not with anything to do with Helen O'Reilly but with sending a threatening letter concerning her landlord, Laurence Brophy. Superintendent Moran was placed in charge of the case. There was nothing for Mamie to do except to face it as bravely as possible. She dressed for the photographers who waited in numbers outside the front door and where a huge crowd now assembled, news of her imminent arrest having spread like wildfire over the city. She put on her light brown fur coat with a gold buckle and brooch. She wore a matching fur hat also with a gold brooch and, carrying her expensive crocodile skin handbag, went down the stairs with the arresting officers. Her outfit was the envy of every woman in Ireland and was talked about for years afterwards. At the front door she posed for photographs. All along the footpath and spilling out on to the roadway the crowd howled at the sight they had been waiting for; they hated Mamie Cadden and they screamed for her to be hanged.

Mamie totally ignored them and even changed the brooch on her lapel from one side to the other so that more photos could be taken. She was certainly putting on a great show for the crowd and for the papers, and she was dressed as all Irish women would have loved to dress in the 1950s: in lavish furs. Nevertheless the photos clearly show that she is an old woman and the bandages on her legs are clearly visible. It all makes one wonder how Mamie could possibly be the potent symbol of sex that she was and remained for the Dublin mob. The papers reported that there were five to six hundred people on the little street to witness the arrest and removal. So many had gathered that traffic was stopped on Hume Street and Ely Place. Photos finished, Mamie was bundled into a waiting squad car while the crowd pushed, whistled and jeered. The car sped off to the Bridewell garda station and later on she was to appear at the Dublin district court where she was returned for trial on charges of threatening the life of her landlord. After that it was back to Mountjoy Jail of which Mamie was all too familiar. She was never to enjoy freedom again.

The fact remained however that the gardaí had insufficient evidence for a conviction. Furthermore the newspapers were filled with articles on the case, all of them hostile to Mamie Cadden. Under today's procedures it would not be considered possible that she could have a fair trial given the hostile media comment but in Dublin's poisonous atmosphere at the time she was already judged guilty and deserving of hanging. At the trial her defence counsel said that she was found guilty 'in every public house in Dublin'.[67] What happened was the epitome of bad policing: first of all a decision was taken that Mamie was guilty and then they sought the evidence to prove it. Her arrest on the ridiculous charge of threatening her landlord's life was just a charade to prove to the mob that the authorities were doing something or else was a strategy to ensure that charges would not be dropped because of the small matter of lack of evidence as once she was in custody she could not be released without the attorney-general and the gardaí losing face.

There now followed an interplay between the chief state solicitor's office, the office and person of the attorney-general and the gardaí. The gardaí were pushing relentlessly for a charge against Mamie Cadden. Not only that, they were pushing for a charge of murder. Any question as to the accidental nature of the death of Helen O'Reilly and a consequent charge of manslaughter seems to have disappeared. The attorney-general at the time was Paddy McGilligan, a member of the second Inter-Party government which was made up of Fine Gael, Labour, Clann na Talmhan and supported by the small Clann na Poblachta party and Independents. Paddy McGilligan was a senior figure in the Fine Gael party having served with distinction as a minister in the state's first government. Most famously of all, he had pushed through the Shannon scheme which was to bring electricity to the fledgling state and to place it at the forefront of technology. Besides being a senior counsel, McGilligan was Professor of International Law and Constitutional Law, Criminal Law and the Law of Evidence as well as being Dean of the Faculty of Law at University College, Dublin. He was admired as an intellectual by none other than Noel Browne, whose politics would have been far away from his.

He was now a sixty-seven-year-old veteran and had become very conservative in old age. He was unlikely to take a stand against anything relating to the social teaching of the Catholic Church. In fact it was more likely that he would be at the forefront of promoting the notion of a Catholic state.

This was the man who had said that in time of economic difficulty people may have to die of hunger in Ireland, a remark that would hardly inspire one to expect him to go out on a limb to protect the civil liberties of an elderly abortionist.[68] Furthermore the attorney-general's office, then called a 'department', was a nest of conservative Catholic social teaching. It included among its small staff of lawyers Vincent Grogan, who was later to become the Supreme Knight of the Knights of Columbanus. It is possible that the attorney-general himself was a member of this secret male Catholic organisation.[69] Disturbingly for liberal Catholics it emerged that Archbishop McQuaid was also a member of this organisation along with leading members of the gardaí, judiciary and the political parties.[70] Certainly, the government, like the previous Inter-Party government was riddled with members of the Knights of Columbanus who included not only Fine Gael ministers but also the Labour leader and Tanaiste, William Norton.[71] McGilligan was probably the only one who could have stopped the campaign against Mamie Cadden by refusing to charge her on the evidence available or insisting on a different charge such as manslaughter.

There followed a correspondence between the authorities aimed at securing a case that would convict her of murder – all the letters are headed 'Murder – Mrs Helen O'Reilly'. The chief state solicitor, Donough O'Donovan, wrote to Paddy McGilligan telling him that the gardaí had done a very good job 'despite many obstacles'.[72] He stated that in his opinion the condition of the body and the clothing, the bloodstains, the nature of the instruments found, the statements made by

Nurse Cadden, the surrounding circumstances, the entries into the diary, etc. 'all add up to something very much stronger than suspicion that Mary Cadden, either alone or in concert with another, is the culprit.'

However, he then went on to say that positive identification of the red fibres and hairs found on the body would 'copper-fasten' the case against Cadden. He suggested that expert examination of the hairs and fibres should be expedited, if necessary calling in the help of the London metropolitan police force at Scotland Yard. He was scathing about the value of the statements taken by the gardaí: 'The vast majority of them,' he wrote, 'will, I think, be found irrelevant when it comes to the time for presenting the case.' These must have been very sobering words especially when he concluded his letter with the advice to the attorney-general: 'In my view, no charge should be preferred pending full technical reports on the hairs, fibres, etc.'

This letter, dated 11 May 1956, could have ended the case against Cadden who was still in custody on the charge of threatening her landlord's life. This approach was given further support when McGilligan received similar advice from inside his own office. A memo to him stated:

Attorney-General,
There should be a further examination as suggested by the chief state solicitor in the fourth paragraph of his minute dated 11 May. Pending the result of this examination no charge should be preferred. M.D.
12.5.56.

The M.D. in question was M. B. Daly, a barrister who was a legal assistant in the attorney-general's department.

It was a golden opportunity for the attorney-general to drop the case, to let it peter out for lack of evidence, or even to just pursue the existing charge of threatening her landlord. It was a crucial moment in the life of Mamie Cadden. But the fates were not with her. Two days after receiving the advice of his own official and three days after the advice of the chief state solicitor, Paddy McGilligan made his decision. He accepted the advice on waiting for the forensic reports before charging her but nevertheless indicated that he intended to act on the file prepared by the gardaí and not the method proposed by the chief state solicitor. He wrote:

Murder: Mrs Helen O'Reilly
While the enquiries have been very detailed and searching it is appreciated that further information is awaited from Preston and that further expert examination of and reports on the hairs, fibres, etc. are clearly necessary. Until these come to hand no charge should be brought.
Superintendent Wymes' file is, however, almost complete.
P. McG.
14.5.56.

So, Superintendent Wymes' (formerly Detective Sergeant Wymes) advice was to prevail and not that of his own official or of the chief state solicitor. It is also important to note that McGilligan states that no charges should be brought until the *reports* of the technical examination were at hand. This is quite different from the advice he had received which suggested that no charges be brought pending the *result* of the technical examination – quite a different matter entirely. It seemed that both he and Superintendent Wymes intended to press charges regardless of the technical results. They were just waiting for them to come in. The reference to Preston relates to Helen's ex-boyfriend, James Byers, and the fact that she took quinine tablets while she was there in an unsuccessful attempt to induce a miscarriage.

The chief state solicitor, his advice ignored, now stepped out of the frame and handed over responsibility to his next in command, the assistant to the chief state solicitor, Liam J. Lysaght. It was a remarkable thing for such a high state official to do but knowing his advice was going to be ignored perhaps he saw it as the only practical course of action given the intensity of the feelings surrounding the case. One wonders, though, what would have happened if he had stood his ground and argued the facts with McGilligan. Liam Lysaght, who now took over the case, was more amenable to the mood for prosecution for murder which was shared by the attorney-general and the garda superintendent. Now all the people dealing with the case would share the same aim: the prosecution of Mamie Cadden for murder. Ten days later on 24 May 1956 Lysaght wrote:

Attorney-General,
I re-submit the papers on this matter together with the latest report from the gardaí received by hand today.
In my opinion the evidence available warrants a charge

and the time is now ripe to prefer it. I shall be glad to have your directions.

L.J. Lysaght.

Assistant State Solicitor.

24 May 1956.

Two days later, on Saturday, 26 May 1956, the attorney-general having given his assent, Mamie Cadden was charged with the murder of Helen O'Reilly at the Dublin district court.

The formal charge was: 'Mary Anne Cadden on or about 17 April 1956 in the county of the city of Dublin murdered Helen O'Reilly.' Superintendent Wymes said that when charged and cautioned Mamie had replied: 'I'll say nothing, I'll tell it all to the judge.'[73] The woman was still not intimidated by the official phalanx lined up against her. They now had their quarry; given the hysterical state of public opinion concerning Nurse Cadden at the time, the huge newspaper coverage, and the generally repressive mood in the state, it was highly unlikely that anything other than a guilty verdict would be arrived at. The highest profile case since the state had been founded was about to be entered, bringing fame to the prosecution and the gardaí. The fact that, as the chief state solicitor had advised, there was insufficient evidence in the statements to convict and that technical evidence would be required, didn't seem to matter. Ireland had returned to the savagery of a witch trial of the middle ages.

16

Blind Justice

There now followed a series of remands in custody for Mamie from different courts while the sworn statements (depositions) of the witnesses and experts were taken. These were the statements referred to by the chief state solicitor as 'irrelevant' when presenting the case. The technical evidence was based mainly on the evidence of Dr Maurice Hickey and made a deposition of twenty-two pages. However, in spite of the warnings given by the chief state solicitor that expert advice on fibres be attained, if necessary from Scotland Yard, the main evidence was from the state pathologist. The only other 'expert' brought in was the retired keeper of the Natural History Museum, Dr Patrick O'Connor. His evidence was on the similarities of the fibres found on the clothing of the dead woman and on the mats in Mamie's flat.

Mamie Cadden was again remanded in custody on Saturday, 2 June, before Justice Lennon. She was beginning to show the strains of her long imprisonment and age. She asked the justice to appoint a counsel and solicitor for her. When she was in jail before, in 1939, she explained, she had employed the best lawyers in Europe. On one occasion she had dropped her legal team at the instigation of a man who turned out to be a communist. She asked the judge to appoint a legal team so that this would not happen again.[74] The nation was in the

throes of an anti-communist campaign after the Soviet inva-
sion of Hungary. Justice Lennon was in no mood for such
pleadings and he told her to have her legal team ready to
defend her at the next court sitting.

On 10 July she was again remanded in custody and sent
forward for trial to the Central Criminal Court. In response
to the charge Mamie replied: 'I have nothing to say only that
I deny the charge. As a matter of fact I cannot stand up. I
will have a doctor to prove that at the trial or a specialist too.
I have never even heard of her. That statement is correct.' If
the prosecution thought they were going to get a confession
from Mamie Cadden they were much mistaken. On 13 July
at the Central Criminal Court the case was adjourned to the
next law term on the application of Mamie's defence team
who were looking for time to build a defence for her.

By this time Mamie had found a new solicitor. He was
Stanley Siev, a young lawyer from an immigrant family who
lived just off the South Circular Road in an area nicknamed
'Little Jerusalem' on account of the large Jewish population.
His family had done well and he had opened a solicitor's
practice in Aungier Street near the city centre. He was very
careful about planning his defence and his strategy, being
conscious that this case was to be far from the ordinary; it
would transcend the purely legal and enter areas of ethics
and religion.[75] He was also aware of the atmosphere at the
time and that Ireland was a very religious country both in
feeling and in personality. He wondered later if perhaps the
reason he was appointed by Mamie had something to do with
his being Jewish though he didn't think that at the time. He

was careful to give religious balance to his team: a Protestant, Ernest Wood, was appointed as senior counsel, assisted by Noel Hartnett, who was a Catholic.

Noel Hartnett had played a very important role in the foundation of the Clann na Poblachta political party in the 1940s and had great hope of political preferment when the party entered government in 1948. He contested the general election unsuccessfully as a candidate in the Dun Laoghaire–Rathdown constituency. His hopes were dashed however and after a falling out with Seán MacBride, the head of the party, he immersed himself in his legal practice while retaining his many political contacts and his radical label. He was a virulent opponent of the Knights of Columbanus and in 1954 had called on the government to exact an undertaking from each of its employees that they were not a member of any mutual benefit organisation, either Knights or Freemasons, and argued that unless these societies were curbed it would mean an end to democracy.[76] He was the leading critic of the Knights and as such was hardly likely to receive any favours from them. This might go some way to explaining the hostility between himself and the presiding judge, Richard McLoughlin, during the trial. The lawyers for the prosecution were: Desmond Bell, SC, and James Ryan, BL. The stage was now set for the legal case of the decade: The People at the suit of the Attorney-General versus Mary Anne Cadden.

The fact that the law allowed a charge of murder for a death that was manifestly accidental requires explanation. It was one of the laws inherited from the British administration when Ireland gained independence in 1922. Under the 1861 Offences Against the Person Act, any person who 'unlawfully' used an instrument or any other means whatever to procure the miscarriage of a woman was considered to have committed a felony (a particularly serious crime in the same category as rape or murder). So when a patient died as a result of such a procedure, they were not considered to have died during a medical operation, and so a charge of murder could be brought against the person who carried out the procedure. A charge of murder could possibly carry a death sentence. This punishment was still on the statue book in 1956. Death by hanging would be at the hands of Pierpoint, the British hangman, who would be brought over by the government for this purpose.

The Cadden trial took place before the legalising of abortion in England but even by 1956 the law in England had moved on significantly while in Ireland it had not. This related to the definition of the word 'unlawful' in the act. For many years it remained undefined but in England this changed in 1939 after the famous 'Bourne Judgement'.[77] In that year a surgeon called Bourne performed an abortion on a thirteen-year-old girl who had been gang-raped by soldiers. He did the operation quite openly, possibly to invite a situation that would initiate a change in the law. He was charged under the 1861 Act. Bourne's defence was that he had operated to save the life of the girl and that therefore the operation was lawful. The jury agreed and found him not guilty of the charge. Furthermore the judge ruled that the operation, as it was designed to save the life of the girl, was indeed lawful. Understandably this ruling was to have enormous consequences on medical practice in Britain as doctors now could act when they felt the life of the mother was threatened by a pregnancy.

Nevertheless the charge of murder against Mamie Cadden went ahead. It seems unjust that a person could be charged with murder because of the performance of an act to which the victim had not only consented but had invited this person to perform. Judge Kenneth Deale, writing on the subject five years later pointed out that if an abortionist hit someone during the course of an assault and that person fell and died as a result then he could not be charged with murder but rather with manslaughter. This is because the crime of assault is considered to be in a lower category of seriousness than the crime of abortion. Assault was considered to be a misdemeanour and this was a less serious charge than a felony. The legal difference between a felony and a misdemeanour was not abolished for many years after this case. This was the tortuous legal background that caused Mamie Cadden to face a charge of murder.

It was the social event of the year in Dublin. People used every bit of influence they had with the legal establishment to get seats at the trial. It was held in Green Street courthouse, an historic building which had seen many famous patriot trials including those of Robert Emmett and John Mitchel, something that would have amused and gladdened Mamie. On the morning that the trial began a queue formed right down the street and round the corner. It was the biggest crowd ever assembled for a trial in the memory of the citizens. The only court case that people could mention that had stirred such enormous excitement in the city was the trial of the Invincibles, members of the secret society who had murdered Lord Fredrick Cavendish and Henry Burke in the Phoenix Park in 1883. The vast majority of the crowd seeking entrance to the courthouse were disappointed as it has a very limited public capacity. Nevertheless many who had arrived early in the morning returned in the evening to hurl abuse at the defendant as she was transported in and out of the court. The chant now was a resounding 'Hang the bitch!' whenever Mamie appeared and was truly shocking in its intensity and viciousness. Mamie did have her supporters though, mainly women, just as she had as far back as her 1939 trial.

The choice of judge boded ill for the defence. Now elevated to the bench Richard McLoughlin had prosecuted Mary Moloney and Christopher Williams in the first of the major abortion trials in 1943. They had received very harsh sentences of ten years and seven years respectively. He would show no sympathy with the defence. If the crowds were expecting entertainment and drama then Mamie was not going to disappoint them. She walked to the dock wearing a beaver skin coat and a coloured silk headscarf. She wore dark green eyeshades and to complete the dramatic effect carried a large magnifying glass in her hand. Having pleaded not guilty she said in a weak voice, 'I'm sorry I can't stand', and she was allowed to sit during the proceedings.[78] In spite of the drama of her first appearance Mamie Cadden seemed distracted, almost in a daze during the trial.[79]

Mamie's letter to the revenue commissioners about her landlord, Laurence Brophy, that had got her into so much trouble was to raise its head again. She had sent it by registered post on the day before Helen O'Reilly had visited Hume Street. As it threatened Laurence Brophy it had given the gardaí an excuse to arrest her in April and keep her in custody until May when the murder charge was proffered. Besides the threats against Brophy it had included tirades against what Mamie saw as the many injustices done to her over her lifetime and it named many people in connection with the allegations she made. Two of these people were priests: Fr Cathal McCarthy of Holy Cross College whom she accused of giving her bad advice in 1938 when she was preparing for her trial for child abandonment. He had advised her to drop her legal advisors, Noyk, Lavery and Cooper and engage Charles Boyle and Co.

Cathal McCarthy was now a priest based in Holy Cross College at Clonliffe in Dublin. But he was much more than just a priest whom Mamie had alleged had given her bad legal advice, he was now the diocesan censor for Archbishop McQuaid. All religious tracts were passed through his hands to check their orthodoxy. At a time when censorship was a national preoccupation he was one of the most important clerics in the whole country. When Mamie picked enemies she certainly aimed high!

Even more startlingly she alleged that the woman whose child was abandoned in 1938 was 'the whore' of a Fr Boylan. There is no way to substantiate or rebuff this allegation now. Only two Boylan priests were in Dublin in 1956. They were

Fr Michael Boylan, the parish priest in Iona Road and the Right Reverend Monsignor P. Boylan of Dun Laoghaire, a close advisor to the archbishop and a former rival to him for the position of archbishop itself. Whichever Boylan she referred to, both were very important clerics in 1950s Ireland and neither would have been too happy to see their name in her letter.

Every day during the trial two priests attended and sat in the public gallery facing the jury.[80] Whether this was related to the above allegations is unknown. The enormous power of the priests in the Ireland of the time can only be imagined now in a more secular age but back then only the very brave or the very foolhardy would go against the priests. Such great and once powerful men as Noel Browne, the minister of Health or Charles Stewart Parnell, the leader of the Irish Party, were to realise this to their cost. Both men went against the power of the clergy and were broken as a result. The presence of the two priests just opposite the jury box must have been hugely intimidating for members of the jury. Things had changed since 1939 and indeed since 1944 and rate-payers from whose lists jurors were chosen were more likely now to be Catholic. It would have taken a very brave Catholic indeed in 1956 to sit in front of two priests for ten days and not come up with a verdict that would have satisfied them.[81]

The trial opened with all the excitement of a huge dramatic presentation. From the outset it became obvious that the state was prepared to make an enormous investment in this trial and would stop at nothing to seek a conviction. The defence too seemed well equipped for its task and gave

Mamie Cadden perhaps the most robust defence she had ever had. Unfortunately it also faced the most formidable obstacles. The case for conviction was opened by Desmond Bell. In a highly emotive address he gave the colour and drama that was anticipated. This he said was a highly pitiful case indeed: a tragic young woman was killed in the course of an illegal operation. Her body was then left on the street like garbage.

Bell described the raid on Mamie's flat on the same day as the finding of her body. He told of how the gardaí had found a Higginson syringe. He told the story of how they had found a forceps with a bloodstain on it – bloodstain which the pathologist said was less than a month old. He told of how they had found two specula in a hat box which Nurse Cadden said wasn't opened for years but on which they had found two fresh fingerprints. Most damaging of all he told the court that these were the type of instruments for carrying out an operation of the nature that caused the death of Mrs O'Reilly. The extent to which the prosecution was prepared to go was amply demonstrated when they revealed a scale model of 17 Hume Street and the adjoining Georgian houses that had been constructed by Garda William Boulter.

The first witness to be called this day was Detective Garda Michael Horgan. He was a photographer with the technical branch and produced two albums of photos for the court. It was his evidence in relation to Mamie Cadden's confiscated diary that was most damning for the defence. There was an entry on Tuesday 17 April: '2 a.m. Blue Coat'. But it had obviously been tampered with and by the use of filters Garda Horgan was able to show that it originally read '8 p.m. Black

Coat' and all knew that Helen O'Reilly was wearing a black coat that day. It wasn't conclusive evidence that Helen had been to see Mamie but was fairly strong circumstantial evidence that Mamie had made an attempt to conceal the appointment. However he did say that he had searched the pavement for drag marks to photograph and had found none.

On the second day of the trial a further thirty-two witnesses for the prosecution were called. They included Helen O'Reilly's female drinking companions, her former boyfriends including the Englishman whom we are led to believe was the father of the child she was carrying. It is very hard to understand why some of these witnesses were called or what possible bearing they could have on the charge of murder. They certainly demonstrated the alienation and unstable nature of Helen's life, and if the intention was that this should rub off on Mamie Cadden and discredit her reputation then it may have succeeded.

Other witnesses that day included Mamie Cadden's landlady, the formidable Gertrude Brophy, her son, Liam, who sometimes collected the rent and young Muiris MacGonigal who was coming home from a scouts meeting that night. (He was later to become a government press secretary and director-general of RTÉ). The other tenants of 17 Hume Street were also interviewed. Among these was Mamie's next door neighbour, Mary Farrelly, a woman of seventy-four who worked in O'Neill's public house in Merrion Row. When questioned on the day the body was found she had indicated that she had heard nothing. Now she said that she had heard 'dragging' noises like furniture being moved at 6 a.m. Her change of evidence, just like that of Patrick Rigney, must cast doubt on its truthfulness. She alleged that at 4.45 p.m. on the previous afternoon she heard women's voices coming from Mamie's flat. This evidence was probably unimportant except that Mamie said she was alone and resting at that time.

There was one amusing but highly embarrassing moment for the participants. John O'Leary had been visited by his girlfriend, Mary Whyte, on that night and they told the gardaí of how she went home at a respectable hour. As the investigations proceeded poor Mary, much to her mortification no doubt, was forced to amend her story. She had spent the night with her boyfriend in his flat in Hume Street.

On day three of the case perhaps the most important witness to be heard on that day, and probably the second most important witness in the whole trial after the state pathologist, was the finder of the body, Patrick Rigney. Yet his testimony was seriously flawed. Before he entered Hume Street at all when he was passing down one side of St Stephen's Green he claimed that he had seen a woman crouched over at the spot where he later found the body. To have spotted someone crouching on the footpath while passing this junction would have required him to look left up Hume Street while still driving his van. Even at that it could have only been a split second view up the street yet he claimed that he noticed she had glasses, was wearing something white and had a stocky build. He further claimed that he saw the glint of the sun on her glasses. It was mid-April and it is highly unlikely that the sun was shining in Hume Street at about 6.25 a.m. as the defence was later to prove. But it didn't end there. Rigney then alleged that having found the body beside the railings of No. 15 he heard a sound from below and went over to the railings and looked down into the basement. There he saw a woman looking back up at him. She was standing with her back to the wall.

Bell, the prosecutor, then questioned him: 'Can you give a description of the woman you saw looking up at you?' Rigney replied, 'I think she had fair hair,' to which Mr Bell asked: 'Can you describe any more about it?' and Pat Rigney's answer was: 'It was raised on her forehead – puffed you know.' He asked him if he could say if the woman in the basement resembled the woman he had previously seen crouched on the footpath and Rigney replied, 'No'. The judge then intervened and asked if the woman in the basement was looking up. Rigney replied that she was indeed looking up and that she was wearing glasses. After all this it then emerged that Patrick Rigney had not initially mentioned the story about the woman in the basement to the gardaí. Furthermore he had told a newspaper reporter that it was perfectly bright at the time and he didn't see anyone else in the vicinity. His excuse for not coming up with the story until he came to the district court was that he knew that he would have to tell it then.

Again we have a case of evidence, this time far more important than that of Mary Farrelly being drastically changed. It is possible that the fame and notoriety of the case made people add on bits to increase their own importance. Perhaps Patrick Rigney was fantasising himself into a position of significance. Whatever the explanation, his testimony did inestimable damage to Mamie Cadden. Though he did not identify her as the woman he had seen either in his testimony to the court or in his written deposition his remarks were enough. The woman he saw had glasses and puffed fair hair, just as Mamie Cadden had.

James Kirwin who lived at No. 15 Hume Street also gave evidence on this day. His story too left something to be desired. He said that he had heard something like a sweeping sound in the middle of the night from his bedroom. This was portrayed by the prosecution as the sound of the body being dragged up Hume Street. This would surely not be a sweeping sound even if it happened but a dragging sound. The body was dragged only a small distance. Kirwin had been interviewed by the gardaí in 1951 in relation to the Brigid Breslin case and they didn't think much of his equally dramatic story then when he said he had heard a woman scream on the street at 2.30 a.m. when nobody else did.[82] Conveniently for the prosecution this was not mentioned at the 1956 trial.

Extra spice was added when Standish O'Grady, the Cork Casanova, was called. He had been reported to the gardaí because of his attendance at the previous sittings related to the case and had been interviewed at the district court in July 1956. His evidence was as expected. He swore that he had never met Mamie Cadden in his life. He conceded that he probably was in Hume Street, perhaps to visit a workman of his in the cancer hospital but he was never near No. 17. One cannot help wondering about the lack of pursuit by the gardaí of this man. He was positively identified by two witnesses: John Moran, who lived in the house and his girlfriend, Elizabeth Bourke, as the man that Mamie spoke to in the hallway for over an hour that night. Yet he was let off the hook. Add this to the fact that he was so strongly associated with the sad case of Brigid Breslin who had died under similar circumstances. Standish had been living in the Dublin suburb of Rathmines at 10 Leinster Road West since April. He had left his country home, Carrigeen House near Fermoy in County Cork. Mamie never once mentioned him in connection with the case even though it might have lessened the severity of the judgement against her.

Mick McAuley, the parking attendant on Hume Street, said that he had seen Standish O'Grady enter 17 Hume Street on several different occasions. He gave evidence that he had been invited in by Mamie that night to examine her notice to quit. Yes, she did threaten to cut up Laurence Brophy but he took it as a comic remark rather than a serious threat. Mamie's famous temper came out as Mick described her as being 'in a passion'.

The fourth day started with evidence from Dr Michael Murphy who came over from the cancer hospital to the body early in the morning. The rest of the day was used to give evidence from members of the gardaí. No fewer than thirteen members of the force were called. Though it was all routine stuff about the finding of the body and the protecting of the exhibits, the number of gardaí testifying certainly showed the seriousness of the gardaí in their intention to secure a conviction. Given the respect the jury would have had for the gardaí, this would have had an effect.

Garda Michael Sullivan in the company of another guard, gave evidence of having visited 17 Hume Street that morning and having been let in by Mamie. She took him up to her room and showed them around. He related about the bucket containing liquid in the middle of the floor. He also told about the phonecall which Mamie took while they were there.

Desmond Bell then asked, 'Did you notice anything about her manner on that occasion?' The garda replied, 'she appeared to be quite normal.' The judge intervened and asked the guard: 'Had you known her before that date?' and Garda Sullivan replied, 'Not to see, my lord.' In other words he had been aware of her reputation in Dublin as a notorious abortionist but had not known her personally. That this came from a policeman made it even worse as it indicated a criminal side to the knowledge he had of her. 'Known to the gardaí' is and was a code for possession of a criminal reputation. When the examination had finished Noel Hartnett requested that the jury be asked to leave the room as he had an application to make to the judge. Justice McLoughlin granted the request and the jury filed out of the court and into their room.

When they were gone Hartnett asked that the jury be discharged on the grounds that the prosecution witness had given evidence of Mamie's previous bad reputation, which was in violation of the rules of evidence. These do not allow the prosecution to present such evidence except in exceptional circumstances. McLoughlin's response was: 'I don't think so at all. The garda's evidence was that she appeared to be normal, and in the circumstances acted as a normal person would, and that she talked normally.' It seemed as if the judge was deliberately missing the point so Hartnett reminded him 'I do not know her *to see*, my lord?' to which Judge McLoughlin replied haughtily, 'I won't discharge the jury.'[83] The case must have been very frustrating indeed for the defence.

The day did supply some of the little light relief that the trial provided. Superintendent Moran was in the box. It was he who had arrested Mamie on the charge of sending the threatening letter to Laurence Brophy. Bell asked him about his visit to her flat. 'I don't suppose she said, "Hello, Superintendent Moran"?' to which the garda replied, 'No.'

Bell continued, 'She is very offensive to you?'

'Occasionally.'

Bell continued, 'And was she offensive that day.'

The superintendent replied, 'Not only to me but to other gardaí.'

Bell pressed on: 'And to the public too?'

'Yes,' he continued.

'Anyone who crosses her path?'

'Yes, including solicitors and counsel,' Superintendent Moran quipped.

The fifth day of the proceedings started off with Superintendent George Lawlor giving his evidence. He was the one who confronted Mamie with her own statement and with the items taken from her flat in an effort to provoke a confession. His crowning moment came when he related the story of the forceps. It had a trace of blood on it but the authorities were only able to say that it was less than a month old. They were not able to analyse it any further. Mamie said that she had not used it for any surgical purpose since she had left her nursing-home in Rathmines in 1939. Witness were called to show that she sold the Rathmines house in 1939 and that the forceps was supplied by Fannin's Medical Suppliers not earlier than 1942.

The day ended with the beginning of the evidence of Dr Maurice Hickey, the state pathologist. He was the key witness in the whole trial and it was up to him to prove, in the absence of any hard evidence, that not only could Mamie Cadden have performed the abortion but that no other explanation was plausible. The authoritarian and hierarchical nature of Irish society, particularly at this time, gave enormous respect to a professional with an important position such as Hickey's. However it now appears that what he presented in court, even from the standpoint of the times, appears to be very flawed indeed. It may also be noted that the Chief State Solicitor Donough O'Donovan had advised that 'expert examination' of the hairs and fibres be undertaken and if necessary 'the good offices of Scotland Yard be invoked.'

Dr Hickey's evidence started on the fifth day of the trial and continued right into the seventh day. He began with the cause of death, giving the report of the post-mortem examination that he had conducted himself. His evidence was that Helen O'Reilly died as a result of an air embolism. This was undoubtedly true. He then went on to say that this was the result of the injection of a liquid through the neck of the womb. He considered no other possible cause. But this might not have been the case. In 1951 Bridget Breslin had been found dead from the same cause. The coroner's court found there was another possible cause, that of violent sexual inter-course and the coroner, Donough MacErlean, mentioned this. The explanation was possibly ruled out by Dr Hickey because of the smell of disinfectant from the wall of the womb but could it be ruled out completely? Why, one won-ders, was this not even mentioned in Dr Hickey's evidence?

Dr Hickey continued that because there was no damage done to the vagina or to the neck of the womb, 'The person who carried out the operation did so with some skill.' He then went on to outline how he thought the operation was carried out from the instruments found in Nurse Cadden's flat. An enema syringe (the Higginson), was employed, to which was added a piece of stiff rubber tubing and the nozzle of a second syringe added on. This could be inserted into the neck of the womb that was being held open by the forceps. The injection of the fluid could then take place. The whole operation could be lit by strong lamps also found in the flat. Rather authoritatively he added that these were the only instruments in common medical practice that could be used in an abortion operation by lay people, nurses and midwives. Interestingly, in this list of possible abortionists he had origi-nally mentioned gynaecologists but later amended it and re-moved all reference to his fellow male professionals. He then added to the list in a highly suggestive fashion the profes-sions of nursing and midwifery.

Dr Hickey gave the bulk of the evidence relating to the hairs and fibres. This was a crucial part of the case as it was necessary to link the body to objects in Mamie's room or on her person. There was still no evidence of anyone seeing Helen entering or leaving Mamie's room. On Helen's black coat Dr Hickey says were found eight hairs, three of which matched a fur cape in Mamie's room and five of which were similar to hairs found on Mamie's combs and brushes. They had been dyed blonde and showed signs of waving particularly at the ends. He concluded that the hairs on the brushes and on the coat could have come from the same person. On one of Helen's black shoes was stuck a cigarette butt. On this was stuck one coarse grey hair of the same type as the fur in Mamie's grey and brown fur cape. Mamie's red dressing-gown was now subject to scrutiny and on it were found two dark human hairs which were similar in colour, texture and degree of wave to Helen's hair.

On the stairway of No. 17 the state pathologist also found dark hairs which were similar to Helen's and one animal hair which may have come from Mamie's fur cape. All this evidence certainly built up the case against her. It was far from conclusive however. The defence would deal with the many ways in which these hairs could have been accumulated and the prosecution, in the days before DNA analysis, was unable to prove conclusively to whom the hairs belonged. It was only able to point out strong degrees of similarity.

Helen O'Reilly was wearing a red woollen jumper when her body was found. Amongst the fibres found on it were two animal hairs, one of which matched exactly those of the fur cape belonging to Mamie. A human hair found on it compared to the hairs found on Mamie's brushes. On the mats in the flat a dark human hair was found similar to that of Helen's type. To add to this, Dr Hickey now testified to the finding of fibres on the mats similar to the fibres on the clothing worn by Helen O'Reilly. Furthermore when he examined the fibres from the black overcoat he found that at least half of them were, in his opinion, from the red dressing-gown worn by Mamie Cadden. At the end of his evidence he gave a slide show about the comparison of hairs and fibres. The serious problem facing him however was that it was impossible to prove conclusively that particular hairs or fibres came from a particular person. No definite link could be established and yet this evidence was the cornerstone of the prosecution.

The temperature evidence showed up very serious problems with the evidence of Dr Hickey.[84] He took temperatures on the morning of 18 April and on these figures calculated such important items as time of death and when the body was left on the street, along with variables of these. These calculations would, of course, be approximate as they would depend on variables such as the temperature of the room in which Helen died. Nevertheless, they were vital to the case for the prosecution as they provided a framework for a reconstruction of the death. The major problem here was that the figures on which Dr Hickey based his calculations were wrong. This meant that all his consequent estimates were also incorrect. It was an astonishing series of errors and how he could have been allowed proceed on this basis now defies belief.

The problem arises from the air temperature calculation in Hume Street that morning. Dr Hickey recorded it as 18°C.

Even a layman would know that the temperature on an April morning in Dublin could be nowhere near 18°C unless in the middle of a heatwave. There was no heatwave in Dublin that day. Dr Hickey had misread the temperature and then went on to calculate the time of death on his flawed statistics. Surely the state pathologist would know that it is never 18°C on an April morning in Dublin. When thinking about this one remembers back to the words of the chief state solicitor asking the attorney-general to ensure that expert opinion be sought. He may have had his doubts about Dr Hickey. The defence, of course, checked the temperature with the records taken at nearby Leinster House Lawn. This is the back garden of Leinster House just a three-minute walk away. The temperature recorded here on that morning was 7°C. This is as one would expect the temperature to be on a fine April morning. Hickey had to take his thermometer into court to have it checked and indeed it was shown to be in working order. He had misread it and neither he nor anyone in his office had seen anything strange in making calculations based on an 18°C morning temperature in April. At this stage one would have expected to have an order made by the judge to have this part of Hickey's evidence disallowed but he didn't. This was in spite of Hickey's admission of his mistake.

The defence then began its cross-examination of Hickey. His evidence on the time of death was discredited when the statistics recorded at Leinster House Lawn were put to him. The defence did not contest the cause of death. One important victory for Ernest Wood was when he got Dr Hickey to agree that hairs could not be used as a method for definite identification. Having established this and the questions re-garding the calculations based on the mistaken temperature readings the defence must have been very pleased with its performance.

The only other witness called on this day was Dr Patrick O'Connor, the former keeper of the Natural History Museum, who backed up Dr Hickey's evidence about the similarities between the fibres on the mats from Mamie Cadden's room and the fibres found on Helen O'Reilly's clothes. He merely restated parts of the evidence of Dr Hickey.

On the ninth day the case for the prosecution was now drawing to a close. Superintendent Wymes gave evidence of the arrest and charging of Mamie Cadden on 26 May 1956. She had been in custody for a month at this stage on the Brophy charge which was not proceeded with. Wymes, like Judge Richard McLoughlin and Superintendent George Law-lor, had a background in the 1940s anti-abortion campaign. Wymes and Lawlor had both received substantial promotions since then. He had been among those pushing for a murder charge against Mamie Cadden.

At the end of the ninth day the prosecution rested. There had been nine days of evidence, all of it circumstantial. The most important witness, Patrick Rigney, the milkman who found the body, had changed his story dramatically as had the elderly Mrs Farrelly, Mamie's next door neighbour. The evidence of the state pathologist was inconclusive as regards the identification of the hairs and fibres and was discredited as regards the temperatures he recorded. It was hardly sur-prising that Ernest Wood, the head of the defence team, called for the trial to be withdrawn from the jury for lack of evidence. Judge Richard McLoughlin refused the application.

On the tenth and final day of Mamie Cadden's trial for the murder of Helen O'Reilly the defence witnesses had their say. There were very few of them, a sharp reminder as to the type of Ireland that had produced the trial. Despite all his efforts, Stanley Siev, Mamie Cadden's solicitor, had been unable to get one doctor to testify as to Mamie Cadden's medical condition. She was suffering from severe arthritis, varicose veins and poor eyesight, yet no doctor would testify for her. She had expected evidence from 'a specialist' but none would come forward lest it damage their careers. The defence also wanted a gynaecologist to examine the medical evidence but again none was willing to come forward. The expert witnesses who did testify in her defence – Dr Earl Hackett from Trinity College, Kevin Bolster from the school of cosmic physics, Dr John L. Synge and Stanley Siev – were Protestant or Jewish professionals whose fear of the priests was probably lessened by their membership of their minority religions.

Mary Brown, who was a shop assistant, testified as to the seriousness of Mamie's arthritis and how she walked with a limp. This brave girl was the best that the defence could come up with regarding the state of Mamie's health. Kevin Bolster, a meteorologist, was able to give the correct temperature on that Wednesday morning, thus contradicting the evidence of the state pathologist. Dr John Synge, senior professor at the Dublin Institute of Advanced Studies calculated the time of death based on the new information on the temperatures. If the body was placed in the street at 6 a.m. then he calculated the time of death to be 4.08 a.m. — ironically also incorrect.

It was Dr Earl Hackett of Trinity College who gave the most startling evidence.[85] He had collected hairs and fibres on the street and in No. 21 Ely Place where Helen had stayed for two nights with Thomas Crowe. When these were analys- ed they came up with the very same results as Dr Hickey had achieved with the fibres and dust from Mamie's room. This demolished the technical case for the prosecution based on the hairs and fibres. He also testified that when blood had dried it was difficult to ascertain its age with any degree of certainty. This laid some doubt on the value to the prosecu- tion of the bloodstain on the forceps taken from the flat even though she had lied about the date she bought it. In an un- usual departure, Mamie's defence solicitor, Stanley Siev, gave evidence. He testified that he had great difficulty in getting Patrick Rigney's amended testimony from the gardaí. He also outlined his inability to get a medical doctor or a gynae- cologist to testify for the defence.

The court then heard the closing speeches for the defence.

17

May the Lord Have Mercy

It is one of the sad twists of fate that Mamie Cadden was to have her best legal defence ever at her final trial when extraneous events would ensure that she had the least chance of acquittal. She had been in court twice before and on at least the first occasion could conceivably have been found not guilty.

In 1956 however when she was defended with skill and passion it seems as if the verdict was decided even before the case began. As her defence counsel, Ernest Wood, said, 'She was already convicted in half the public houses in Dublin.' More disturbing though was the attitude of the trial judge, Richard McLoughlin. His conduct during the trial was nothing short of hostile. The evidence against Mamie was very sparse indeed and should not have been sufficient to convince anyone who was not already prejudiced against her. Sadly this must include the jury which, under the strange circumstances and time of the trial, must have found it as almost their religious duty to convict. Stanley Siev, Mamie's solicitor, put it well when he said: 'This was a case in which legalities were passed over and it moved into issues of ethics and religion.'[86]

Now with the summations the hostility of the judge to Mamie was to rear its ugly head again. It was Wednesday, 31

October 1956, and the final day of the trial.

Ernest Wood summed up the case for the defence. It was a mighty effort: Nurse Cadden had at last found an advocate worthy of the drama of the situation. Wood spoke for an astonishing six hours. Appealing to the jury's sense of fairness he said that she had already been convicted by 'the Dublin Whispering Gallery' because of her reputation and before the facts in the case were known. The time of death as adjudged by Dr Hickey and his mistaken calculations was disputed. His scientific deductions in relation to the hairs and fibres were unreliable in that the same or similar results were recorded six months later from debris from the street and from Thomas Crowe's flat in Ely Place. Wood argued that the evidence of Patrick Rigney and Mary Farrelly was unreliable. Both had changed their stories significantly. Rigney had given testimony that had been easily contradicted: namely when he said that he had seen the glint of sunlight on the glasses of the woman he saw in Hume Street when the sun would not have been on the street at that hour of the morning.[87] Mrs Farrelly said that she had heard a 'dragging' sound in the morning. It had stopped when John Moran the unemployed baker had gone out in the morning and started again after he left. If this was the case, he said then Moran must have stubbed his toe on the body on the stairs!

Wood argued that a woman of Mary Anne Cadden's physical condition would not have been able to take the body down two flights of stairs, down a hallway, out the door and up the street past two houses. His client was suffering from arthritis and was incapable of such a strenuous task. This seems like an unanswerable argument. It was a problem though that Wood could not get a doctor or consultant to testify to this but he did mention these circumstances.

When Wood had finished Noel Hartnett closed the case for the defence and brought up many interesting points. Wood had spent his time undermining the case for the prosecution. Hartnett now outlined a possible alternative scenario: perhaps the body had been dumped on Hume Street because the real abortionist knew, as so many did, that Nurse Cadden lived there and that suspicion would fall on her. The syringe had been free from all smells or traces of disinfectant. How then could it be believed that it was used in the operation? The ownership of the scarf around the neck of Helen O'Reilly could not be traced to her or to Mamie Cadden. Who owned it? The red umbrella found beside the body had a fingerprint. This was neither Helen O'Reilly's nor Mary Anne Cadden's. Whose was it? As for the hairs found on the red dressing-gown, the gown had been removed in a garda van that was frequently used for collecting drunks from the street and the hair could easily have been transferred on to it from there. It all added up, he argued, to a set-up by the real abortionist knowing that Nurse Cadden would be the number one suspect: 'The old woman has a blotted escutcheon [reputation],' he argued, 'and was an easy mark for suspicion.'[88] He finished up with the memorable phrase that there was not enough evidence in this case against the defendant 'to hang a dog'.

James Ryan gave the case for the prosecution. The person, he said, who dragged the body to 15 Hume Street was the murderer. He made a remarkable allegation. Referring to the testimony of Patrick Rigney he said, 'He has been man enough to say that the woman he saw was the accused woman in the dock.' But Rigney had not said that at all. When he had finished Noel Hartnett rose to his feet, repeated Ryan's remarks and asked the judge to discharge the jury because of them.

The judge replied, 'He did not say it, Mr Hartnett.'

A shocked Noel Hartnett asked, 'Mr Ryan didn't say it, my lord?'

The judge said, 'No,' but Hartnett replied, 'Well, I jotted it down in my notebook.'

'Will you tell me what he did say?' asked the irritated Hartnett.

The judge replied that Mr Rigney had said that was the woman and the woman was the murderer. An exasperated Noel Hartnett then repeated his request: 'I ask you to discharge the jury.'

Judge Richard McLoughlin almost admitting Hartnett's charge said, 'I will of course make it right,' meaning that he would ask the jury to disregard the statement by Ryan.

Calming down somewhat Hartnett said, 'You say that even if he did say it, it does not matter? Is that your lordship's ruling?'

The judge, glad to be let off the hook replied, 'Yes.'

But he didn't set the record straight and never corrected the impression that Rigney had identified Mamie Cadden as the woman he saw in the basement and neither did he refer to the matter in his address to the jury. Justice McLoughlin summed up by explaining the case as he saw it to the jury. He said that where a death was caused by an act of violence due in the course of, or furtherance of, a felony, malice was implied by law. It did not matter, he said, that the person committing the act did not desire the death of the person or that the person against whom that act was committed had consented to that act being committed.

In this case, he continued, the evidence was such that he thought that the jury must come to the conclusion that on or about 17 April some person caused the death of Helen O'Reilly by using an instrument or another means to procure an abortion which was a felony by statute. His summing-up in effect reduced the case to an abortion case. If there had been an attempt to procure an abortion then a murder had been committed. He was the best ally the prosecution had in the case.

The jury retired at 7.30 p.m. to consider the evidence. It was recalled when Ernest Wood, obviously stung by the judge's remarkable summing up, asked the judge to explain some points of law to it. He asked the judge to clarify the nature of circumstantial evidence in relation to a guilty verdict. Judge McLoughlin explained to the jury that to find a guilty verdict on solely circumstantial evidence they must be satisfied that the facts were inconsistent with any other explanation. This would explain Hartnett's approach as he painted a possible alternative reason for the body on the street.

There was another vivid interchange between Wood and the judge to do with the whole basis of the charge of murder.

He asked if there was any other verdict but murder open to the jury. The judge replied without hesitation, 'My view is that there is but one verdict on the one count open to the jury.'[89] That was clear enough. Nurse Cadden was to be found guilty of murder or found innocent of murder. The jury had no difficulty or delay in reaching the verdict. It took them a mere hour. They returned at 8.45 p.m. and the foreman, James Hodgins, read out the verdict of the twelve: Count No. 1 – Mary Anne Cadden on or about the seventeenth day of April 1956 in the County of the City of Dublin murdered Helen O'Reilly. Hodgins gave the verdict 'Guilty'.

Before he delivered his sentence Judge McLoughlin told the jury that he agreed with their verdict![90] He then went on to refer to allegations against the state pathologist who had misread his own thermometer and based a whole range of calculations on the incorrect data. 'Any criticism of the state pathologist,' said the judge, 'I regard as without foundation and unjustified.'

Mr Justice Richard McLoughlin then asked the customary question of Mamie Cadden: 'Has the defendant anything to say why sentence of death should not be passed on her?' If he thought this was going to intimidate her he had made a serious mistake. Mamie spoke for the first time during the case. She was calm, cool and collected. Looking straight at the judge she said, 'You will never do it. This is not my country. I am reporting this to the president of my country. This is the third time I am convicted in this country falsely. And I will report it, and I will see about it at a later date. Thank you. Only for my counsel I would say something you would not like to hear.'

The judge now signalled for his black cap, he placed it on his head and gave his verdict: 'The sentence and judgement of the court are [sic] and it is ordered and adjudged that you Mary Anne Cadden be taken from the bar of the Court where you now stand to the prison whence you last came and that on Wednesday, 21 November in the year of the Lord 1956, you be taken to the common place of execution in the prison in which you shall be then confined and that you shall be then and there hanged by the neck until you are dead and that your body be buried within the walls of the prison in which the aforesaid judgement of death shall be executed upon you.'

While the verdict was being given women in the public gallery sobbed loudly. Outside on the packed street it was a different story. When news of the sentence filtered out there was wild cheering as the mob jumped and danced with joy and screamed: 'Hang her! Hang the bitch!' Even now Mamie showed the almost manic courage and contempt for authority that was the hallmark of her entire career. When the judge finished his sentencing with the customary phrase given after the passing of a death sentence 'and may the Lord have mercy upon your soul' she was in, quick as a light with, 'Well, I am not a Catholic. Take that now.'

Ernest Wood was on his feet. Whatever about his feelings about the fairness of the proceedings he now asked in a respectful tone for leave to appeal the sentence of death. Judge Richard McLoughlin refused the application. He thanked the jury and recommended that they be exempted from jury service for twelve years. Thus proceedings ended and Mamie Cadden, to the cheers of the mob, was taken back to Mountjoy Jail to await her execution in less than three weeks' time.

18

'This Wretched Creature'

It was a matter of the greatest frustration and anger to Mamie's defence team. On the face of it, they could not foresee how their client could have been found guilty with such a lack of evidence but they were only too aware of the background to the trial. The potent mixture of religious and legal prohibition of abortion and the distinct whiff of illicit sex around the case ensured the 'guilty-of-murder' verdict even before the meagre evidence was presented. For her legal team it was a nightmare. It seemed that no matter what defence they presented it would make little difference. Their only hope lay in the law which provided a small but real protection for outsiders and minorities since the state had been founded. On this ground if on no other they must appeal the sentence. Having been refused in the Central Criminal Court, their next step was to go to the Court of Criminal Appeal.

The preparation for the appeal involved some visits to Mamie in Mountjoy. Stanley Siev went there with a typist. The soft-spoken solicitor recalls his shock at Mamie's 'blue' language during his visits and how embarrassed he was that this language was used in front of his female typist! Mamie denounced her tormentors in no uncertain terms. The woman, far from being intimidated and cowed by her sentence, now lashed out. In December of that year the medical officer in Mountjoy Jail, Dr Murphy, reported that she was 'an extremely garrulous person with an especial animus against those who administer justice and the Catholic clergy'.[91]

The Wednesday following the sentencing the appeal was ready and presented by Siev. As the applicant it was of course signed by Mamie herself – her signature was now one shaped by arthritic pain, so much different from the earlier copperplate writing that she shared with her father. There were seven reasons presented; five of which concern Judge Mc-Loughlin 'misdirecting' himself or the jury in points of law. The reasons were:

1. That the learned Trial Judge's charge as to the nature and effect of circumstantial evidence and its application to the evidence was insufficient and confusing to the Jury;

2. That the learned Trial Judge misdirected himself in law in refusing to discharge the Jury on the application of Counsel for the accused;

3. That the learned Trial Judge misdirected the Jury by directing them that they could consider evidence of similarity of hairs and fibres as evidence implicating the accused in the offence charge;

4. That the learned Trial Judge introduced or permitted to be introduced evidence which was not on deposition and of which no notice had been furnished to the accused;

5. That the learned Trial Judge misdirected himself in law in ruling that it was not open to the Jury to find the accused guilty of manslaughter;

6. That the trial was unsatisfactory;

7. That the verdict was against the evidence and the weight of evidence.

These were fairly serious grounds and stinging indictments of Judge McLoughlin. While it was unlikely that his fellow judges would come down hard on him at least they would be free from some of the pressures facing the jury in the Central Criminal Court. Nevertheless it was an age in which it is still believed that the tentacles of the Knights of Columbanus extended deep inside the legal profession.

There was another major problem facing the defence. Mamie had now run out of money. Siev applied for free legal aid (an application that was allowed for in criminal cases) on 7 November, the same day as he lodged the appeal. Part of the gossip machine about Mamie had been about the large amounts of money she earned for her services. In an impoverished society this generated great jealousy and hostility. But Mamie's outward show of prosperity hid the squalor inside 17 Hume Street and the enormous amounts of money she paid to the legal profession over the years.

The registrar of the Court of Criminal Appeal to whom the request for legal aid was made contacted the garda commissioner to ascertain what means were at Mamie's disposal.[92] Superintendent Wymes writing to his superior, the commissioner, indicated that at the time of her arrest, which was in April 1956, she had about £1,000 in a Dublin bank. Now just seven months later she had 'no more than £100 to £200 to her credit'. In other words she had spent about £800 in legal fees for the case at the Central Criminal Court. This was an enormous amount of money then. The application was granted and she also received free transcripts of the evidence for her counsel.

On 23 November 1956 leave to appeal was granted. To give some flavour of the times an item on the same page of the *Evening Mail* that was reporting the upcoming appeal also informed its readers that from Vatican City on Friday came the news that 'The Pope had a good night's sleep'. Seemingly he rested well during Thursday night and worked as usual during Friday though 'he had been suffering from a slight attack of influenza'! It was hardly indicative of an atmosphere that would release Ireland's last surviving abortionist.

The Court of Criminal Appeal was presided over by Chief Justice Conor Maguire, Mr Justice Teevan and Mr Justice Murnahan. The case was taken in the last full week of the law term before Christmas. The arguments of the defence were refined and re-stated: the problem about the time of death based on a misreading of the temperature by the state pathologist; the difficulty about identifying hairs and fibres when all the prosecution could prove was a similarity with fibres in Mamie's room; the problems with the changed testimony of Patrick Rigney and Mary Farrelly; the dependence on circumstantial evidence; and the failure of the judge to correct a statement by the prosecution that Patrick Rigney had identified Mamie Cadden as the woman in the street on the morning he discovered the body.

As if all this weren't enough the defence made a strong argument that the jury could have reached a verdict of man-slaughter and that Judge McLoughlin's direction to them to the contrary was wrong in law. This was a very serious point as to concede it would question Judge McLoughlin's ability to preside at a murder trial. Thus the appeal became as much a trial of Richard McLoughlin's suitability as a judge as it did of Mamie Cadden's murder verdict and sentence. The Appeal Court was to choose between the establishment, including a fellow judge, and a notorious and 'garrulous' nurse.

The appeal ended on Saturday, 22 December 1956, and Chief Justice Conor Maguire announced that he would give the verdict on Monday 24, Christmas Eve. Even the defence team didn't expect a reprieve for their client in the middle of the holy season of Christmas that was so deeply based on family values and Christian teaching.

They were right. Chief Justice Conor Maguire, in dismissing the appeal, upheld as correct Judge McLoughlin's directions to the jury. The judge was also right, he ruled, when he said that it was not open to the jury to return a verdict of manslaughter. As for Rigney's evidence and the allegation that he was purported to have identified the accused, the court ruled that the judge's whole treatment of the evidence showed a studious and obviously deliberate avoidance of any suggestion that purported to identify the accused.

The whole appeal had been a terrific waste of time and money. The defence received no satisfaction on any point. The court would not criticise Judge McLoughlin on any issue not to mention overturn the trial.

It was Christmas Eve and their lordships fixed the new date for the hanging of Mamie Cadden. It was now to take place on 10 January 1957.

There was now a race against time. A woman had not

been executed in Ireland since 1925 when Annie Walsh of Fedamore, County Limerick, had been hanged in Mountjoy Jail for the murder of her husband. However, given the anti-Mamie hysteria, it was now not inconceivable that such an event would take place again. It would certainly please the mob and the more extreme religious sections of the community. As the whole apparatus of the state closed down from Christmas Eve to St Stephen's Day time was running out.

On the day after St Stephen's Day Stanley Siev wrote to the attorney-general asking that the manslaughter issue be referred to the Supreme Court where 'the law on this matter should be definitively decided'. The attorney-general, himself a legal expert, nevertheless sought advice from his own department. What he got back must have been a bombshell. The memo he received read: 'On the more modern trend on England it does seem that a verdict of manslaughter might have been returned'.[93] However as is usual in memos such as this the opposite argument is also made. This device is used so that the minister or in this case the attorney-general has scope to make a decision either way. The advice here is that in older cases then a verdict of murder is justified. As for the appeal to the Supreme Court the official whose initials are E.D. advises that the point of law is hardly of exceptional public interest but to wait for the report of the Court of Criminal Appeal before he makes up his mind.

It was Friday, 28 December 1956, and no decision would be made that week. On New Year's Eve 1956 the news was that an appeal to the Supreme Court would not be entertained by the attorney-general. There would now be no legal redress for Mamie Cadden. The conviction and sentence would stand.

The liberal lobby in Ireland in the late 1950s was very weak on the ground. There were very few appeals to the government for clemency and they came only from very brave individuals and one organisation, the Irish Association of Civil Liberties. This small group, founded in 1947, included such brave defenders of liberalism as the writer Sean Ó Faoláin and was to the forefront in fighting the draconian censorship laws in the country. Only one member of the Oireachtas asked for a reprieve: Senator Owen Sheehy-Skeffington, son of the pacifist Francis Sheehy-Skeffington – who had been murdered on the orders of a British army captain during the 1916 Rising; and Hanna Sheehy. Sheehy-Skeffington wrote to the Taoiseach John A. Costello on New Year's Day 1957. He wrote that he was 'morally certain' that the cabinet would commute the sentence. Hanging her, he suggested, would lose our society 'a measure of self-esteem and degrade itself'.

The Irish Association of Civil Liberties also wrote in favour of a reprieve. Their Honorary Secretary Edgar M. Deale wrote to the secretary to the government on 3 January: 'Since in our view the whole trend of modern opinion is that only deliberate killing merits the title of murder, and further, as the Government has recently indicated that it will consider the revision of the law, we respectfully suggest to the Government that they should in the meantime recommend a reprieve in the Cadden case.'

Next into the fray was Stanley Siev who wrote on behalf

of Mamie herself. It is unlikely that he checked the contents of the letter with Mamie herself as he wrote: 'She is of abnormal mentality and while it is not suggested that this amounts to a degree of insanity exempting her from criminal responsibility, it occasioned considerable thought and anxiety to her advisors as to whether she was legally fit to plead. It is suggested that this abnormal mentality deprives her of the normal appreciation of her moral and criminal responsibilities.'

He also attached a list of signatures for reprieve, which he says, were sent to him unsolicited. This is an amazing record of the civil libertarians in Ireland in 1956–57. One of the great surprises is the number of Church of Ireland notables. This is difficult to explain outside their own feelings for justice or perhaps they were influenced by Ernest Wood, Mamie's defence counsel. The list includes Canon Simpson of Clyde Road, Canon Frederick L'Estrange also of Clyde Road, four members of the Simms family of Clonskeagh and Mr Armstrong, the Rector of Howth. Other signatures included Oisin Kelly the sculptor, Austin Clarke the poet, Sheelagh Johnston the actress and mother of Jennifer Johnston, and John Keegan of Kilard, Kilbeggan, County Westmeath, a War of Independence veteran whose son, Sean, would become an arch-conservative Fianna Fáil TD. There were a mere seventy-one signatories. The president received seven letters in all relating to the reprieve.

Credit for the reprieve must go to the government which, as already noted, was a coalition between Fine Gael, Labour and Clann na Talmhan supported by Clann na Poblachta. It was led by John A. Costello who was a senior legal figure in his own right. The government resisted calls for the implementation of the death penalty in this case, perhaps even from some of its members. On 4 January 1957 it made the necessary recommendation to the president and Nurse Cadden's sentence of death was commuted to penal servitude for life.

19

'If It Wasn't for Helen O'Reilly'

Mamie was unrepentant. She never accepted the judgement of society, the courts, the gardaí or the Church that her work as an abortionist was evil. This position would not have been considered to be extreme forty years later but in the 1930s, 1940s and 1950s it was believed to be a deeply subversive position deserving of the greatest of punishments including death by hanging or life imprisonment. The only regret she expressed before her death was that she had been caught.

In June 1957 she made her will with a new solicitor, Brendan Boushel, who practised at 12 Ely Place, quite near her old flat in Hume Street.[94] He was later to become one of the richest men in the state when he became a major share-holder in the pharmaceutical corporation, Élan. In 1957 it was a different story however as he drew up the will of the convicted murderer, Mamie Cadden. She appointed as her executor and beneficiary her cousin, Paddy Cadden, a carpenter who lived in a flat at 63 Lower Leeson Street. She did not mention her other cousin, Patrick Martin, of 29 Beaumont, Drumcondra who is mentioned in the prison register as being her next of kin though her brother, Joe, was still alive at the time. Neither did she mention her onetime friend, Standish O'Grady, though we can safely assume that self-serving Standish had dropped her first. Her scrawly handwriting shows a further deterioration in her arthritis even since the previous November when she signed the form to appeal her death sentence. When she died her estate and assets were valued at £250.

Paddy had been involved in some lively correspondence with the attorney-general. He had written alleging that Mamie's landlady, Gertrude Brophy, had broken into Mamie's now empty flat and removed property belonging to her. The truth of the allegation was not contested by Mrs Brophy. It is not known what happened to Mamie's collection of furs and jewels which she had collected over the previous thirty years. In the next decade the house was let out to three students, Michael Conaghan, Eamonn Maloney and Dessie West.[95] It was Eamonn Maloney who found the two boxes of medical instruments hidden in what had been Mary Farrelly's flat. They were obviously hidden there by Mamie shortly after the death of Helen O'Reilly when Mrs Farrelly was at work. This means that the police exhibits at the trial were unlikely to have been the instruments used by Mamie in her last operation. Maloney, now a Labour party councillor, proudly keeps a jug and basin, once the property of Nurse Cadden, as a souvenir of those years.

The Dublin mob that cheered at her death sentence didn't forget Nurse Cadden as she languished in Mountjoy Jail. The stories about her were legendary. Biddy White Lennon, the well-known television actress who lived in the vicinity, said that when she walked past 15 Hume Street her mother used to point to the house and tell how Cadden used to strangle girls there with nylon stockings.[96]

Mamie's health deteriorated rapidly during these months in prison. Despite her age she was still subjected to the rigours of penal servitude as ordered in her sentence. Mysteriously, in 1958 she was declared insane. This meant that this difficult prisoner could be transferred to the Central Criminal Lunatic Asylum in Dundrum as the Central Mental hospital was then known. All who knew her however, are emphatic that she was not insane. One theory says that she was transferred to Dundrum because she was quite ill with a heart condition and the medical services there were superior to those in Mountjoy Jail. The Dundrum facility is set in grounds and the regime is more relaxed there and would be more suitable for a terminally ill person than the prison regime in Mountjoy Jail. If this theory is correct then it was one of the only kindnesses shown to Mamie Cadden by the authorities and reflects well on Seán Kavanagh, the governor of Mountjoy, who is remembered as a humane person.

Was Mamie Cadden insane or was she confined to the asylum in Dundrum to ensure that she would never reveal the names of her clients or the doctors who referred their patients to her? Was she sent there because she was a quarrelsome old woman whom the governor of Mountjoy wanted rid of? The transfer papers from Mountjoy have been misplaced and the prison authorities refuse to answer or acknowledge any query about their former inmate. The governor at the time, Seán Kavanagh, would have had responsibility for the prison records and their safekeeping. Here another problem arises as it emerges that Kavanagh was a leading member of the Knights of Columbanus, the organisation that often seems to crop up when we look at the final years of Mamie Cadden.

The asylum authorities refuse to release her file and the East Coast Area Health Board supports this refusal for the reason that 'the release of these records would not respect the rights to privacy of third parties'.[97] The national archives too had a file on Mamie Cadden in its Department of Health section. This has also gone missing.

In any event she was transferred to Dundrum in August 1958. She was assigned to what was called an 'epileptic bed' and her arrival there is still remembered as a major event in the history of the institution. Dr William J. Coyne was the resident physician and governor of Dundrum and was obviously quite annoyed at having this notorious patient foisted on him.[98] On the day of her committal to Dundrum he said in the hearing of other staff members: 'This woman isn't mad.'

Mamie soon became a most popular inmate in Dundrum with the young staff who worked with her. She became especially friendly with three young girls who were carers in the asylum. The matron was a strict disciplinarian and was rigid about the rules she expected staff and inmates to obey. Mamie immediately christened her 'Hairy Mary' and covered for the staff when they might get in trouble with matron. Once the young girls working there brought a Hula Hoop into the wards and they all had a go while Mamie Cadden stood guard at the door ready to give the signal in case 'Hairy Mary' should arrive.

She was already known to one of the girls as she had treated her for dandruff two years earlier. She regularly laughed and joked with them. One girl who was a bit more brazen than the two others innocently and jokingly asked her 'If we wanted an abortion, would you give us one?' Mamie laughingly replied, 'Go away from me; you couldn't afford one.' Each evening she was given a bottle of stout and she particularly enjoyed this. It was a far cry from the treatment she had received in Mountjoy Jail. The past and her incarceration continued to haunt her. She often talked to herself and sat alone in a hut in the grounds of the asylum. One of the girls who had befriended her heard her say one day: 'Only for bloody Helen O'Reilly I wouldn't be here.'

She died peacefully in her wicker chair on Monday, 20 April 1959. It was 2.45 p.m. and one of the young attendants was with her. She just fell back dead in the chair. The girl said the Act of Contrition into her ear in line with Catholic custom. When he heard the news Dr Louis Clifford, the assistant resident medical officer, said: 'There's many thanking God that she is gone as their names won't be mentioned now.' The post mortem was carried out on her the next day on behalf of the Dublin county coroner, Dr James Brennan by Dr J. O'Gorman of 25 Rathgar Road.[99] She states that Dr Coyne, Dr Clifford and Miss E. Pogue were present when she died. Her death certificate lists the cause of death as 'Arteriosclerosis, Myocardial Degeneration, Pulmonary Infarction'.[100]

After the post-mortem she was laid out in a cheap coffin and prepared for burial by two of the girls who had befriended her in Dundrum. They cried as they washed and dressed her for her final journey. She was buried in Deans-grange Cemetery in County Dublin.[101] She rests there in the St Nessan's section in a plot owned by the Dundrum Central Criminal Lunatic Asylum. It is a mass grave for those who died in the asylum. The interred are not given even the dignity of having their own names recorded on the grave. The headstone reads: 'Central Mental Hospital + Rest in Peace'.

It had been speculated in the papers that her family might bring her back to the family plot in the graveyard near Lahardane for burial. Her brother, Joe, was still alive, in fact he was just fifty-eight at the time. It was not to be, however, undoubtedly the notoriety of the most famous member of their family must have been too much for them. Joe did arrive at the asylum and collected her effects, including a black record book she had. There was great speculation among the staff that this book would contain Mamie's lists of clients and doctors who had referred patients to her. This is highly unlikely, however, as one of Mamie's most valuable traits was her confidentiality and discretion. Her diaries did not name her clients but as we know from the 1956 trial indicated their identity by an article of clothing.

So we end the story of Mary Anne Cadden, one of the most remembered and controversial Irishwomen of the twentieth century. Perhaps she was the most hated woman of twentieth-century Ireland by those who deplored her profession and her ethics. But what of the thousand plus women who came to her in desperation when all else had failed them? How many mother's lives did she save? Which of those women has ever condemned her? How many are living today because of her intervention?

Now more than a hundred years after her birth she is still a topic of conversation and controversy in Ireland. In Dublin it seems that everyone over sixty has a story to tell about her. To many of her relatives her life is still a taboo subject. In the year 2000 she first appeared on the Internet when a woman reported ghostly sightings of newborn babies on a lonely Meath road and connected them with Nurse Cadden.[102] This must have been based on a jumble of the stories of the child abandonment case near Dunshaughlin and the false story of the bodies in her back garden in Rathmines. It is still told that the clocks in the asylum at Dundrum all stopped at 2.45 p.m. on the day that she died. Her remarkable life story certainly left an impression on the Irish people that will not easily be erased.

17, Hume Street,
Stephen's Green,
Dublin.
16/4/56.

To The

Revenue Commissioners,
Dublin Castle.

Dear Sirs,

Please find enclosed the said "Receipts without Stamps."
When I demanded on more than one occasion He Brophy told me that
the State and I could go to hell. I enclose the stamped
receipts of £16.5.0. plus £15.8.9. for April, 1955. Mrs. Brophy
demanded £4.0.0. increase. I said, If the Law says Yes I will do
it. If not "NO". As you can see the Law said my lawful rent was
£5.14.2½ in lieu of £16.5.0. The lowered it to £15.8.9.
because I said I would not pay that amount because Brophy told
me at first that he was supplying light. The E.S.B. cut off the
light as Brophy would NOT pay his Bill. I also got my Name
Plate and Bell on door at my expense. On the 10th day of January
1956, the Plate and Bell were damaged. I called the Police.
They asked if I had any Suspects. Yes said I The "Landlord" as
he was mad when the rent was fixed by the Justice including
Name Plate and Bell also light, but at my expense. "(I lost
£50.0.0. worth of a watch in the Dark by Brophy." Brophy billed
me with a Demand Note of £35.14.0. for his Rates and Taxes
I said get out you "Pig". 1944 I was jailed for 5 years for
Having Doyle, 26, Frankford Park, Dundrum, and his Whore Ellen
Thompson, Abortion done by Larry Doyle with a piece of lead
piping, & Hat pin, of which I withhold in my Bank. If Doyle
did not do it why did he Doyle pay me the sum of £54 odd by an
order of the Court? I am going to charge the State for False
Imprisonment on 11 Charges. I have concreate evidence.

                                        M.C.

P.S.

I have had my share of Father McCarthy, Holy Cross
College, Dublin, in 1938 for Father Boylan's whore
plus her Bastard that was dumped by Kathleen McLoughlin, 7,
Berkly Road, Dublin, in Dunshaughlin Road. He McCarthy pointed
his gun in Mountjoy Jail on the 23rd day of July, 1938. He said
Desperse with your Solicitor and Counsel in 48 hrs - or your
life is in Danger, namly Noyke Lavery & Hooper and that I was
to secure Boyle the "Free Mason" and his son Vssay & McCarthy
Counsel & Dye your hair black. I should have shot him dead,
when he poked his Pig's Snout in my Private Affairs. IIII
certainly NOT. He thinks he will get me out. NO until he
walks on my "DEAD Body." I have paid my rent fixed by the Law
& I will pay "no more" He returned the Rent of £8.4.11. sent
by my 'Bank' Manager the 14th inst. paid 3 mths in advance,
ending the 13th day of July, 1956, No Dirty "Underground
Communist" can do that. "Irish Landlords" If he comes in here
to throw me out, I will shoot him dead and also put the Butcher
Knife to the Handle in his Pot Belly.

                    Signed
                    "Nurse" Cadden N.S.A.

Appendix: Mamie's 1956 letter to the revenue commissioners

Notes

1 See Mamie's letter to the revenue commissioners.
2 Coroner's report on death of Brigid Breslin, 1951.
3 Report from Superintendent M. J. Wymes to the District Commissioner, 13 November 1956.
4 Interview with Cathal O'Shannon, 30 January 2002.
5 Deposition of John Moran taken on 11 June 1956.
6 Church records from St Peter's Cathedral, Scranton, Pennsylvania.
7 Land Registry Office.
8 1901 census.
9 The 1901 and 1911 census returns indicate Mrs Mary Cadden's ability to read and write, yet when registering her daughter's death in 1925 she signs with an X.
10 Information from the midwifery tutor, National Maternity Hospital.
11 Central Statistics Office.
12 Registry of Deeds.
13 Statement of Kathleen McLoughlin, 1 August 1938.
14 Statement of Margaret Berkery, 30 July 1938.
15 *Irish Independent*, 15 July 1938.
16 Interview with a friend of Mamie Cadden's who wishes to remain anonymous.
17 Deposition of Sergeant Robert Gough, 8 July 1938.
18 Dail Fireann, Official Reports, 1935.
19 Dr David Nowlan quoted in R. S. Rose's thesis.
20 *Pro Life? The Irish Question* by Michael Solomons (Dublin: Lilliput Press, 1992).
21 Exhibits at the Central Criminal Court, 1–5 May 1938.
22 *Daily Mail*, 18 July 1938.
23 *Irish Independent*, 11 July 1938.
24 Letter from the chief state solicitor to the attorney-general, 20 September 1938.
25 Letter of Mr Boyle to the attorney-general, 20 October 1938.
26 Statement by Francis Vanston, 26 October 1956, at the Central Criminal Court.
27 Registrar of Births, Marriages and Deaths, Castlebar, County Mayo.
28 Letter from Director of Midwifery/Nursing, the Rotunda hospital, to

the author in 2002.

29 *Irish Times*, 19 May 1939.

30 Female register, Mountjoy Jail, 1939.

31 Letter from the attorney-general, Kevin Haugh, to the chief state solicitor, 10 September 1940.

32 The bulk of this story is based on the deposition of Ellen Thompson given on 6 December 1944.

33 Deposition of Dr John McGrath, the state pathologist, 15 December 1944.

34 R. S. Rose's thesis: *An outline of fertility control focussing on the element of abortion in the Republic of Ireland*, 1976.

35 Charge sheet of William Henry Coleman, 1944.

36 *Evening Mail*, 2 June 1944, and on many other occasions.

37 Exhibits in the Coleman case included his Register of Patients.

38 Testimony of Mr Mifsud, 1944.

39 *Evening Mail*, 30 November 1944.

40 The State Book at the Circuit Criminal Court, 1941–45.

41 Interview with Brendan Ashe, a relative of Thomas Ashe.

42 *Irish Times*, 1 August 1944.

43 *Irish Times*, 26 October 1943.

44 Evidence of Olive Myler, former secretary of the Central Midwives Board.

45 *Irish Times*, 22 December 1944.

46 Deposition of Dr John McGrath, the state pathologist.

47 For Mamie's letter see appendix.

48 Female register, Mountjoy Jail, 1945.

49 Female register, Mountjoy Jail, 1945.

50 *The Work* by Fergal Bowers, Poolbeg Press, 1989; and *The Knights of St Columbanus* by Evelyn Bolster, Gill and Macmillan, 1976.

51 Interview of Standish O'Grady by Garda Inspector T. O'Brien, 25 June 1951.

52 Coroner's inquest on Brigid Breslin, 1951.

53 Deposition of Mick McAuley at the 1956 trial.

54 Department of Justice files, 1938.

55 *Dublin Historical Record*, Vol. LV, No. 1.

56 The last three weeks of Helen's life are outlined in the report of Superintendent Wymes to his district commissioner dated 13

November 1956.

57 *Sunday Press*, 29 April 1956.

58 Evidence of Mick McAuley, 24 October 1956, at Central Criminal Court.

59 In the famous 1925 case of the murder of prostitute Honour Bright, a suspect, Dr Purcell from Blessington, admitted having sex with her in Hume Street.

60 The deposition of Patrick Rigney, the date it was taken crossed out.

61 Detective Garda M. Horgan, the garda photographer, said at the trial: 'I was looking for a drag mark but did not find any.'

62 She was seen by Chief Superintendent Farrell.

63 The deposition of Dr Maurice Hickey, the state pathologist, taken on 18 June 1956.

64 Deposition of Garda Michael Sullivan taken on 15 June 1956.

65 Attributed to John Lawlor, youngest son of George Lawlor, by Tom Reddy in 'Murder Will Out' from Kevin O'Connor's *Thou Shalt Not Kill*, Gill and Macmillan, 1994.

66 In his letter to the district commissioner of 13 November 1956 Superintendent Wymes states categorically that Mamie's male visitor that night was Standish O'Grady.

67 Closing remarks of Ernest Wood at the 1956 trial.

68 Attributed to Paddy McGilligan in Noel Browne's book, *Against the Tide*, Gill and Macmillan, 1986.

69 The convention among the Knights was that the name of a fellow Knight could only be divulged with his permission.

70 *The Knights of St Columbanus* by Evelyn Bolster, Gill and Macmillan 1976.

71 *Ibid.*

72 Files of the attorney-general, 1956.

73 *Sunday Press*, 27 May 1956.

74 *Sunday Press*, 9 June 1956.

75 Various interviews were conducted with Stanley Siev, starting on 7 February 2002. Now in his eighties, Siev continues to practise as a solicitor.

76 *The Knights of St Columbanus* by Evelyn Bolster, Gill and Macmillan, 1976.

77 R. S. Rose's thesis.

78 *Evening Mail*, 22 October 1956.

79 Interview with Gerry Callanan who attended the trial.

80 Stanley Siev interview, 7 February 2002.

81 The court records of the trial come from the National Archives, supplemented by the records held in the office of Stanley Siev.

82 Coroner's inquest on Brigid Breslin, 1951.

83 *Beyond Any Reasonable Doubt* by Kenneth E. L. Deale published by Gill and Macmillan, 1971.

84 *Cork Examiner*, 30 October 1956.

85 Dr Hackett was also the pathologist to the Adelaide hospital, 1955–57.

86 Interview with Stanley Siev, 7 February 2002.

87 Cross examination by Ernest Woods.

88 *Cork Examiner*, 30 October 1956.

89 *Cork Examiner*, 30 October 1956.

90 *Evening Mail*, 2 November 1956.

91 Department of Justice files, 'Briefing to Government', 1957.

92 Court records, Court of Criminal Appeal, 1956.

93 Attorney-general's files, 1956.

94 The last will and testament of Mary Anne Cadden, the National Archives.

95 Two of the three occupants of the house went on to become Labour Party councillors: Michael Conaghan and Eamonn Maloney.

96 Biddy White Lennon interviewed by Gavin Corbett in 1998.

97 Letter from the board to the author in refusing a Freedom of Information Request, 2002.

98 Much of the information on Mamie's stay in Dundrum is based on an interview with a friend of hers who does not wish to be identified.

99 Coroner's inquest on Mary Anne Cadden, 1959.

100 Death certificate of Mary Anne Cadden.

101 Information from Deansgrange Cemetery.

102 Blather Archives on the internet. It includes comments from a local priest and from Caroline Lane, Mamie's grand-niece.

Bibliography

Bolster, Evelyn, *The Knights of St Columbanus* (Dublin: Gill and Macmillan, 1976).

Bowers, Fergal, *The Work* (Dublin: Poolbeg Press, 1989).

Browne, Noel, *Against the Tide* (Dublin: Gill and Macmillan, 1986).

Cooney, John, *John Charles McQuaid: Ruler of Catholic Ireland* (Dublin: The O'Brien Press, 1999).

Corbett, Gavin, *Nurse Cadden and the Irish Backstreet Abortion Trade* (Dublin: Trinity College, 1998) unpublished thesis.

Deale, Kenneth E. L., *Beyond Any Reasonable Doubt* (Dublin: Gill and Macmillan, 1971).

Jackson, Dr Pauline, *A Deathly Solution to an Irish Problem* (Dublin: Women's Right to Choose Campaign, 1983).

— *Abortion Trials and Tribulations* (Dublin: UCD Women's Studies Forum, 1987).

— 'Outside the Jurisdiction – Irish Women seeking Abortion Abroad' in *Gender in Irish Society*, (Galway: Galway University Press, 1987).

Kelly, David M., *Bloody Women* (Dublin: Gill and Macmillan, 1999).

O'Connor, Kevin (ed.), *Thou Shalt Not Kill* (Dublin: Gill and Macmillan, 1994).

O'Shannon, Cathal, 'Cadden and the Body in Hume Street', from the *Thou Shalt Not Kill* series (Dublin: RTÉ television, 1994).

Prone, Terry, *Irish Murders* (Dublin: Poolbeg, 1992).

Reddy, Tom, *Murder Will Out* (Dublin: Gill and Macmillan, 1990).

Rose, R. S., *An Outline of Fertility Control, Focussing on the Element of Abortion in the Republic of Ireland* (Sweden: University of Stockholm, 1976), unpublished thesis.

Solomons, Michael, *Pro Life? The Irish Question* (Dublin: Lilliput Press, 1992).

Whelan, Gerard and Carolyn Swift, *Spiked – Church–State Intrigue and The Rose Tattoo* (Dublin: New Island, 2002).

Index of Names